Information Literacy WITHDRAWN

Search Strategies, Tools & Resources for High School Students and College Freshmen, Second Edition

Zorana Ercegovac

Linworth Books

Professional Development Resources for
K-12 Library Media and Technology Specialists

Library of Congress Cataloging-in-Publication Data

Ercegovac, Zorana, 1947-
  Information literacy : search strategies, tools & resources for high school students and college freshmen / Zorana Ercegovac. -- 2nd ed.
      p. cm.
  Includes bibliographical references and index.
  ISBN-13: 978-1-58683-332-9 (pbk.)
  ISBN-10: 1-58683-332-4 (pbk.)
  1. Library research--United States. 2. Information retrieval. 3. Information literacy. 4. Report writing. I. Title.
  Z710.E72 2008
  025.5'24--dc22

                                    2008001893

Cynthia Anderson: Editor
Carol Simpson: Editorial Director
Judi Repman: Consulting Editor

Published by Linworth Publishing, Inc.
3650 Olentangy River Road
Suite 250
Columbus, Ohio 43214

ISBN 13: 978-1-58683-332-9
ISBN 10: 1-58683-332-4

5 4 3 2 1

Table of Contents

List of Figures and Tables

Chapter 9: Citing in Style and Summarizing

List of Exercises

Chapter 1: Introduction to Basic Research Skills
Chapter 2: Finding Search Words
Chapter 3: Search Strategies
Chapter 4: Fact Finding: Words, Concepts, Events, Places
Chapter 5: Fact Finding: People, Reviews, Criticism

Chapter 6: Finding Works in Library Collections

Chapter 7: Searching & Evaluating Internet Sources

Chapter 8: Finding Magazine and Newspaper Articles

About the Author

Dr. Ercegovac earned her Master's in Ethnomusicology (1973) and MLS (1975), both from the University of Illinois at Urbana-Champaign. She then moved to California and worked as a consultant and educator before deciding to go back for her doctorate (UCLA, 1990).

She has published widely in premier scholarly journals, including *Journal of the American Society for Information Science and Technology* (JASIST), *Information Processing and Management, Annual Review of the Information Science and Technology* (ARIST), *Cataloging & Classification Quarterly, College and Research Libraries, Library & Information Science Research, Reference Librarian, School Library Journal, KnowledgeQuest*, and many others. She was the guest editor of the November issue (1999) of JASIST on metadata. Most recently, Dr. Ercegovac was invited to contribute an article to the *Encyclopedia of Library and Information Science*, edited by Marcia J. Bates and Mary N. Maack, on the topic of plagiarism. Her research has been supported by prestigious funding agencies, such as the National Science Foundation (NSF), Online Computer Library Center (OCLC), Engineering Information Foundation, and the Library of Congress (American Memory Fellowship, 2001).

Dr. Ercegovac has contributed in the area of information literacy research and practice. After she had taught hundreds of college students at UCLA for many years, she was convinced that information literacy does not start at the college level. It starts much earlier. Her classroom experience with college students, 7-12 students, and other populations, has confirmed her belief that there is a commonality among information seeking behavior regardless of searchers' age and individual differences. In 1995 Ercegovac found an IL consulting firm, InfoEN Associates focusing on collaborative and problem-based learning and curriculum-embedded information literacy.

Acknowledgments

The greatest contribution to this work has come from my family: my daughter Una read numerous versions of the entire manuscript (for the first edition) many times, and contributed as an editor and consultant. My son Vuk asked important questions and clarified technical issues. My husband Miloš D. Ercegovac contributed to all technical, many conceptual, and affective aspects of the work.

I wish to thank Marlborough School, especially Barbara Wagner, Head of School, who has supported me in numerous ways throughout this project (since 2005). Collaboration with teachers at Windward School (1998-2005) contributed to the writing of the first edition of this work (Ercegovac, 2001). I am grateful to Linworth Publishing, specifically to Marlene Woo-Lun for her continuous support and encouragement, and to Cynthia Anderson for her understanding and fruitful discussions, especially in July of 2006. Appreciation must go to anonymous reviewers, who generously donated their time in reading and critiquing this manuscript. I wish to thank UCLA's Department of Information Studies for giving me the opportunity to teach a 4-unit undergraduate information literacy course, as well as several other graduate level courses (1991-1998).

Information Literacy

Search Strategies,
Tools & Resources for
High School Students
and College Freshmen,
Second Edition

Preface
to the Second Edition

Goal and audience

This expanded and updated second edition has been designed as a practical guide to
information literacy programs for high school students and college freshmen. It will
be especially useful to instructional librarians, as well as to high school and college
instructors as a guide to teaching information literacy skills and concepts.
Professional development and in-service programs will find this edition useful in
planning and researching the way experts do, critical thinking skills, and ethical
uses of information. In addition, schools of education and information studies may
want to use this book as a baseline stock of skills to orient future educators to
accessing a wide variety of resources and knowledge organization techniques.

Unique features of the second edition

This book builds on the strengths of the earlier edition (Ercegovac, 2001). In order
to enhance students' lifelong learning, collaboration, and application of learning
standards in interdisciplinary contexts in high schools and college settings, my
three-prong approach embraces:

- **_Holistic treatment of educational standards._** Information literacy standards, titled _Standards for the 21st-Century Learner_ (American Association of School Librarians), information technology (International Society for Technology in Education, _National Educational Technology Standards_), and content (with performance) curriculum standards are treated as composite rather than fragmented stand-alone standards. In reality, there are more overlaps than differences between and among the existing standards (see Appendix A: Alignment between information literacy and technology standards). For details about our main goals and means to achieve the goals, readers may want to consult Appendix B as well as Boyer Commission (1998), Ercegovac (1999; 2003b), Manduca & Mogk (2002), _Science Teacher_ (2004), and Williams (2003).

- **_Gap-bridging aims toward high school-college transitioning._** We have separate standards for K-12 and college levels (see Appendices A and B). How do we bridge gaps between elementary and middle school, from middle to upper school, and from there to college? By mapping different standards, especially focusing on authentic inquiry-based projects at the intersection between high school and college levels, we hope to make these gaps narrower and transitions seamless and relevant. Examples will be given in appendices in the back of this book (see Appendices D through G; also see Ercegovac, 2003a).

- **_Layered learning._** Assuming that students, instructors, and librarians will all be users of this book, we offer a layered approach to information. In some cases, instructors may use this book as a required textbook in their Information Literacy (IL) classes; however, in other cases, the instructor may use some of the reproducible appendices and think guides for their students. Most of this book will be a common stock and applicable to all readers. However, some of the sections will be more relevant to students and others will be more useful to instructors. For example, "College libraries are not just larger school libraries" (Appendix C), is especially relevant for high school seniors transitioning to colleges and universities.

Users' experiences and feedback from the first edition (Ercegovac, 2001) are factored into this second expanded edition; some areas are updated in terms of new resources and URL addresses. Over the past eight years, we have seen a new wave of Information Literacy (IL) put in place as best practices in schools and colleges; evolving educational technologies, along with proliferation of "social machines," have influenced new modes of seeking, searching, learning, and using information technology. These areas have been expanded and woven into the existing text.

Here are several scenarios that illustrate various uses of this book for interdisciplinary collaborative research projects; the examples below support the three-prong approach just described (e.g., _holistic_ approach to curricular, IL, and Information Technology (IT) standards; _transitioning_ from high school to college, and _layered_ presentation of information).

- **Scenario 1:**

  The honors science class is preparing independent research projects in small groups of two to three students per group. Librarians and technology coordinators are unable to always customize their instructional units to meet individual project needs. Science instructors use appropriate sections of this book as a resource for their own preparation. For examples, see lesson samples from Appendix E that can be modified and individualized to local needs; students read pertinent sections that relate to a wide range of resources (See Appendix D on primary sources and digital libraries; see also relevant appendices on how we organize knowledge in high school and college/research libraries, Appendix H1, H2). All users consult sections on how to use evidence to support claims and cite sources (Chapter 9; see, Think Guide #6 on Honor Principle). Using a variety of IT tools, students present their research methods and findings as interactive posters, conference paper proposals, and write papers in collaboration with local university mentors. Cited references with abstracts are a part of their posters. Drawing on helpful strategies and examples that are given in this book, teachers use fewer scaffolding techniques ensuring that students have appropriate IL and IT skills, tools, and sources. As students get more confident, the frequency of prompts may fade away.

- **Scenario 2:**

  A career related workshop resulting in individual student portfolios is one of the projects that most students are motivated to work on and get ready for their next step. Students use a wide variety of sources for professional awareness and preparation. Students research potential areas of interest for possible careers and share with other students their findings at school career fairs. They prepare Web pages, establish and moderate blogs, and produce other types of information that can be updated and interactively maintained. Supervised by their advisors, students work independently on their own portfolios and consult this book for first best sources (e.g., *Occupational Outlook Handbook* <www.bls.gov/oco/>, *Encyclopedia of Careers and Vocational Guidance*, College Board, Peterson's series of handbooks for colleges and schools, magazines such as *CareerWorld*, to mention just a few widely used sources). Other chapters, appendices, and Think Guides are consulted as needed during the different phases of preparation. Think Guides are hands-on exercises involving both concepts learned in the preceding chapter and critical thinking skills.

- **Scenario 3:**

  Students present museum podcasts to interpret exhibits with audio and video explanations for teens. The term podcasting is defined as a method of distributing multimedia files, such as audio programs or music videos, over the Internet using either the RSS feeds or atom syndication formats for playback on mobile devices and personal computers. Other students develop museum programs for parents and other audiences of their choosing (e.g., senior citizens, blind persons, and pre-K children). For each project, students conduct research seeking characteristics and needs of their visitors in order to better design program guides and museum catalogs. Students use ARTstor database <www.artstor.org>, National Portrait Gallery <www.npg.si.edu>, or local museums to draw upon images for their projects. Students podcast and develop methods that they would use to monitor the success rate of their products in order to iteratively improve ease of use, effectiveness, and language. The project pulls together multiple talents, tasks, and subject contents. Students need to define their goals, users and uses, required resources, assessment techniques, collaborative skills, and work with art teachers and librarians at different phases of their projects in order to succeed in making the recreational use of IT an educational one with a strong learning component. See Appendices F and G for examples of projects in the arts and social sciences.

- ### Scenario 4:

  During summer months, for in-service activities, and orientation of new faculty, students, and staff, instructional librarians work with instructors to showcase:

  - New capabilities in specific services, databases, portals, and systems;
  - Search tips for specific projects and departments of newly acquired databases, such as the ARTstor online image database, *JSTOR*, and *Grove's Dictionary of Music and Musicians*;
  - Programs that can be used in classrooms, homes, labs, art studios, and libraries.

  By working closely with the faculty, instructional librarians learn firsthand about new projects, ideas, and strategies that are beneficial to the entire learning community.

Organization

This book is divided into nine chapters. The first three chapters are of general nature and apply to research planning and searching techniques and strategies, regardless of the format or medium (Chapter 1). We search by means of selecting search words— What are they, where to find them, and how to use them. Is there any difference between "keywords," "title words," "subject headings," and "concept" searching? Answers to these questions are in Chapter 2. Whether you search Web-based magazine and newspaper articles, Internet sites, or library catalogs, you need to know certain basic skills and search techniques that apply across all of these sources (Chapter 3). Think Guides #1 through #3 provide additional opportunities for students to explore the material presented in each of the corresponding three chapters. In Chapter 9, we show how to cite and summarize sources that you will include in your own reports or presentations. As importantly, we elaborate on the reasons for attribution in academic communication. Think Guide #6 includes an example of the Honor Principle that can help prevent plagiarism and foster academic honesty in general.

Chapters 4 through 8 include various resources in the order these sources are typically used in the process of library research. The assumption is that students are novices (such as high school students and college freshmen). Chapter 4, *Fact Finding: Words, Concepts, Events, Places* covers dictionaries and encyclopedias, as well as maps, atlases, and gazetteers. Chapter 5, *Fact Finding: People, Reviews, Criticism* covers related resources regardless of their medium, e.g., printed (by Gale), or online (through InfoTrac by Gale Group). Chapter 6 is on online library catalogs: what they are, which questions are appropriate in using library catalogs, and how to use them. In contrast to the first generation of online catalogs, this edition will draw on Web-based library catalogs that are point-and-click object-oriented and more consistent with Web-based online databases, search engines, and digital libraries. Chapter 7 is on Internet resources. An important part of this chapter covers the best practices in evaluating sites that are typically not peer reviewed and may be content inappropriate, fake, or developed for commercial purposes. Think Guide #4: Evaluation of Web Sources, offers criteria to aid in thinking critically about Web contents. Chapter 8 is on accessing a variety of magazine and newspaper articles. We present a current trend among online products and services that were once available only to higher education customers. Many producers have widened their markets and made it economical for high schools to subscribe to their databases (e.g., Web-based *Encyclopedia Britannica, World Geography Index, CultureGrams Online, CQ Press E-Library* online collections, *Oxford English Dictionary, Grove's Dictionary of Music and Musicians, ProQuest, EBSCOhost, SIRS*, Gale Cengage databases, *JSTOR*, ARTstor, and many others). Think Guide #5 (how to critically read articles), along with Appendix N (how to summarize) offer a framework to help students organize information into "new knowledge." These headings may be applied when reading a paper from an online database, newspaper story, a chapter in a book, or a biographical essay.

This author has covered most of the chapters in a five–week period. Special features of this book include six Think Guides and 17 Appendices that supplement and enhance individual chapters described in Table P1.

The information literacy program that is described in this book is *comprehensive* because it:

- Contains references to a variety of sources and digital collections.
- Introduces effective information literacy search strategies and tools for the use of these sources.
- Covers critical evaluation of these sources.
- Considers *Information Power: Building Partnerships for Learning* (1998) as well as *Standards for the 21st-Century Learner* (2007).

Chapter	Appendix	Think Guides (TG)
Preface to the Second Edition	A: Alignment between IL and technology standards B: Goals and means C: College libraries are not just larger school libraries	
Chapter 1: Introduction to Basic Research Skills. Inquiry-based lesson plans are given in Appendixes D through G.	D: Getting started with primary sources E: Lesson plans in the sciences F: Lesson plans in the arts G: Lesson plans in social sciences	Think Guide #1: Topic Narrowing Exercise
Chapter 2: Finding Search Words	H1: Dewey Decimal Classification H2: DDC<->LCC crosswalk	Think Guide #2: Finding Search Words
Chapter 3: Search Strategies		Think Guide #3: Search Strategies
Chapter 4: Fact Finding: Words, Concepts, Events, Places		
Chapter 5: Fact Finding: People, Reviews, Criticism		
Chapter 6: Finding Works in Library Collections	I: IL Baseline pre-test J: Scoring rubrics	
Chapter 7: Searching & Evaluating Internet Sources	K: Post-test—An example of take home final quiz	Think Guide #4: Evaluation of Web Sources
Chapter 8: Finding Articles in Online Databases	L: Online databases M: Self-reflection (can be used throughout the book)	Think Guide #5: Thinking Critically about Articles
Chapter 9: Citing in Style & Summarizing	N: Summarizing sources	Think Guide #6: Honor Principle
Bibliography	O: Cited reference sources P: Evaluation of reference sources	

Table P1: The overall organization of this book

Within this one-stop information literacy mall, the program also features **45 figures** and **tables**, **29 exercises** and more than **180 selected Web sites, digital libraries,** and **high quality portals**.

The book is *tested* in classroom and computer lab settings with students who had little or no information literacy skills. Collaborative work with teachers in history, science, foreign languages, and the arts, has helped this work evolve into a curriculum-integrated and project-supported program.

The book is *flexible*: the content is divided into a series of interrelated yet independent chapters. This means that you do not have to start with Chapter 1, proceed sequentially to Chapter 2, and end with Chapter 9. However, starting off with Chapter 1, which covers some basic library and research skills, may help as your first selection.

How this book can help educators (instructors, librarians, technology coordinators):

1. This book has its basis in empirical research, and has been validated in a real classroom environment with high school and college students. Instructors' feedback has been incorporated as well as the school reform standards.

2. The author has had classroom experience both in high school curriculum as well as in college instruction. She has seen first-hand what students need to know before they come to college. She has also seen successful college students who had come from secondary schools with well-thought-out IL programs. All of them had been exposed to frequent library use, research process, and IT skills. **If you want your students to graduate with information literacy skills, this book is for you**.

3. The book lists printed resources (in Appendix O) and describes more than 180 Web sources throughout the book. These will be maintained and kept current via this author's home page <http://infoen.net/research>. The bibliography identifies and cites around 70 major works in the various aspects of information literacy theory, practice, and assessment techniques.

4. This book will help justify an Information Literacy program to administration. No one wants to be left behind; schools want to produce excellent graduates, to see them succeed in the colleges of their choice. This book will assist you in this regard.

The book translates research from information-seeking behavior, the information search process, information retrieval, and educational psychology into a practical information literacy program for instructors, media specialists, students, and parents. The book will ensure that our high school graduates, wherever they go and whatever they pursue, will be well prepared, informed, and self-motivated for the lifelong learning journey ahead.

Conceptual Framework: of special interest to instructors

The conceptual framework for this work draws on learning theory, research on information seeking of young adults, and information literacy within school reform.

For the selected reading list on information literacy models, learning and assessment reports, as well as other relevant texts, readers are referred to the bibliography in this book.

Learning theory

The information literacy approach taken in this book considers the five components of learning: content understanding, problem solving, self-reflection, collaboration, and communication.

For details, see Center for Research on Evaluation, Standards, and Student Testing (CRESST) reports, work by Kuhlthau, Pitts, Small, and works in various disciplines in the bibliography in back of this book.

This book includes six Think Guides and 17 appendices. These are designed to highlight each of the five learning components. The Think Guides contain worked-out examples that may be adapted and distributed to students.

Table P2 illustrates how each of these five learning components of higher level thinking is linked to information literacy skills and specifically to chapters in this book.

While researchers such as Kuhlthau have focused on the importance of motivation and affective variables in the information search process, Small discusses the Attention, Relevance, Confidence, and Satisfaction (ARCS) model that library media specialists can use to motivate student learning in integrated information literacy units. Among research questions, Small has studied types of motivators that are used by library media specialists. She found that middle school library media specialists (LMSs) used more extrinsic motivational strategies (e.g., verbal praise) than intrinsic strategies (e.g., curiosity, contextualization, and challenge). As we move toward upper school grades and college settings, we have opportunities to motivate students to apply research skills, critically evaluate materials, and ethically use information in their work. An example is self-selection of research projects on topics of students' interest rather than on the topics of their teachers' interests.

Research on information seeking of young adults

The information seeking process (ISP), according to Kuhlthau (1997; 1999a; 1999b, 2004), incorporates the experience of interactive thoughts, actions, and feeling in the process of construction. Thoughts relate to the cognitive domain, such as problem solving; actions relate to the sensory-motor domain such as scrolling and navigating through the Web; and feelings relate to the affective domain, such as uncertainty, clarity, interests, likes, dislikes, and motivation.

Learning Components	Links to Information Literacy Skills
Content understanding	Students learn to see the Big Picture and consider multiple sources across all formats and media; they learn to ask a question and shape their project focus; to differentiate access locators, and to learn characteristics of information sources. Students as PLANNERS (Ch. 1, 4-8, Think Guides 1-6 + Appendices)
Problem solving	Students learn to organize their "think pads", plan their search strategies, and find search terms. Students translate assigned projects to information need, major concepts, and learn to break concepts into search words (Ch. 1-3, + Think Guides 1-5). Students as PROBLEM SOLVERS.
Collaboration	Students work in small teams to brainstorm, evaluate, present, and peer-teach. Teachers and media specialists collaborate together on IL units. Students as TEAMWORKERS (throughout the book, especially Appendixes D-G).
Self-reflection (self-regulation)	Students monitor their progress and timing, improve their planning, research process, responsible use of information, search strategies, and correct errors. (See Appendix M and Think Guide 6).
Communication	Students communicate their findings via written projects, presentations, creative works, and annotated bibliographies. They learn to use information and information ideas ethically (Appendix N). Students as SCHOLARS.

Table P2: CRESST Model of learning linked to Information Literacy skills, Chapters, Think Guides, Appendices

More recently, information seeking researchers have investigated secondary school students' behaviors in the digital environment. Of particular relevance to adolescents' searching patterns are studies conducted by Agosto (2002), Agosto and Highes-Hassell (2006), Chung and Neuman (2007), Griffiths and Brophy (2005), Dresang (2005), Hughes-Hassell and Miller (2003), and meta-analyses by Todd (2003).

For example:

- Griffiths and Brophy found that 45 percent of students in their study's sample used Google as the search engine of choice.

- In her work with school children, Bilal discovered that most children liked ease of use of electronic over print sources, ability to search by keyword (versus subject headings), amount of information the Web offers, availability of images, convenience, and fun (2000).

Urban teens' everyday life information seeking has been studied by a growing number of researchers.

- Studies by Agosto and Hughes-Hassell (2006), Savolainen (2004), and Shenton and Dixon (2003) report a wide range of teens' information needs.

- Agosto and Hughes-Hassell's model of urban teens' everyday information-seeking suggests that the teens use various resources to meet their information needs; the resources include people, computers, television, books, newspapers and magazines, radio/CDs, telephones, and so on.

All this has wide implications for us as educators to design appropriate contents and interfaces, and to integrate information literacy skills and concepts into school-based curriculum so that teens can be properly informed about their topics of interest ranging from academics to popular culture, health, social/legal norms, career opportunities, sexual and cultural identity, civic duty, and familial relationships. **As more plentiful resources become available to us, it becomes more essential to teach critical thinking skills as well as ethical uses of information ideas.**

Information literacy within school reform

Some of the above findings are applied in "*A Position Paper on Information Problem Solving*" prepared and endorsed by the American Association of School Librarians <www.ala.org/aasl/positions/PS_infolit.html>. The position calls for increasing the partnership between teachers and media specialists in order to collaboratively create integrated and resource-based learning experiences. **The phrase "resource-based" learning refers to the ability to create knowledge based on the evidence from multiple resources; students learn to access, locate, interpret, analyze, and apply evidence in order to achieve specific goals**. A goal might be to prepare a travel brochure of a particular geographic and cultural region; to take opposing views on a particular historical issue and link it to a current event or phenomenon; or to create a visual, three–dimensional diorama, PowerPoint presentation, radio and television broadcast, RSS feed, wiki, blog, or Web document. The position paper embraces the restructuring of our schools. This component has not been well incorporated in many existing information literacy models and programs.

More work is needed to link higher level cognitive demands with curricular frameworks and assessment instruments. Finally, we do not have, as yet, well-defined alignment between and among multiple components of the educational environment, such as standards, assessments, texts, resources, quizzes, lecture notes, lab notes, and class plans. However, *Standards for the 21st-Century Learner* (2007) demonstrates that we as a professional community have come closer to achieving the common goal: to facilitate students' lifelong learning. The title of the standards embraces the underpinnings of this work that was laid out in the earlier edition (Ercegovac, 2001).

In order to help your students become efficient information users and lifelong learners, we have developed *Information Literacy: Search Strategies, Tools & Resources for High School Students and College Freshmen*, a comprehensive, classroom-tested, curriculum-integrated, flexible, and project-based information literacy resource. The book takes a student-centered perspective rather than a technological perspective. **It focuses on helping students understand various ways information is organized in order to find a relevant level of sources for their inquiries. We focus on the intellectual aspects of locating, interpreting, evaluating, and communicating information sources, rather than on the technical aspects of these activities.**

Zorana Ercegovac, Los Angeles, 2008.

CHAPTER

Introduction to Basic Research Skills

In this chapter, you will learn how:

- To think about finding information of interest that will become useful in your projects throughout your high school and college years
  - understand basic ways information is organized
  - learn to use a variety of information sources regardless of format or medium
  - identify characteristics of information sources
- To ask a good question
  - recognize and express information needs
  - focus on the topic of your choice
- To use research language effectively

Chapter 1 introduces the different ways information is organized and searched. It discusses important characteristics of information sources that experts find useful in locating information. This chapter shows how to express information needs and translate the need to a good question. It is necessary to begin by defining the essential concepts (e.g., access, locate, ask, and meanings of library catalogs and online databases) that will help you become an educated information user.

To *access* means to retrieve a record representing a physical document. For example, when we search library catalogs, we see many different types of records. These records, despite their differences, typically include the author's name, title of an item, and subject headings; the physical description of an item and publication information may also be given. Through these data elements, records describe physical documents such as books, CDs, or DVDs. To *locate* means to retrieve an item, either physically or electronically. An item may be a book, a map, a photograph, or a film; each piece may be printed on paper or available digitally, such as a printed book and its electronic version.

In the example of Franklin of Philadelphia, the author is *Esmond Wright*; the title is *Franklin of Philadelphia*. Subject headings are: *Franklin, Benjamin, 1706-1790*; *Statesmen—United States—Biography*. This means that we can look this book up in the library catalog by the author's name (search under esmond wright in either order), title words (use significant title words, franklin philadelphia; ignore the preposition "of"), and subject headings (any combination of the words in the two subject headings).

Notice that the words in the publication and description fields are not searchable (see Figure 1.1). However, we can browse library shelves in the 973.3092 area (according to the Dewey Decimal Classification, which you will learn in Chapter 2) for biographies of persons who lived in Colonial America. You may find biographies of many prominent early Americans including Adams, Franklin, Hamilton, Jefferson, Marshall, Paine, Revere, and many other famous names all grouped together in the same general area in your library.

Author: Wright, Esmond
Title: Fanklin of Philadelphia.
Publication: Cambridge, Mass.: Belknap Press of Harvard University Press, 1986.
Physical description: xvii, 404 p., [18] p. of plates : ill. ; 25cm.
Notes: Includes bibliographical references and index.
Subject headings: Franklin, Benjamin, 1706-1790.
                       Statesmen--United States--Biography.

Call number: 973.3 WRI

Figure 1.1: Cataloging entry for Wright's *Franklin of Philadelphia* book

To *access* and *locate* writings by and about Benjamin Franklin, use any of the following retrieval systems, preferably in the following order:

- **Reference sources** typically include dictionaries, encyclopedias, almanacs, yearbooks, directories, and gazetteers; an example is the multi-volume *World Book Encyclopedia*. If you are looking for an article on Franklin, make sure your volume includes the letter F on its spine (F for Franklin). The entire *Encyclopedia* is arranged alphabetically; that is, articles on topics, places, events, and people are all arranged alphabetically, from A to Z. The last volume contains an index that shows articles on Franklin throughout the multi-volume set. To learn more about encyclopedias, go to Chapter 4. Some encyclopedias, such as *Encyclopedia Britannica* <school.eb.com> are available by subscription on the Web. We will spend more time distinguishing content from an interface later (in Chapter 4, Fact Finding, and in Chapter 7, Searching and Evaluating Internet Sources). Often, students tend to believe that if a content is accessible through the Internet, it is trustworthy; another myth is that they do not have to cite information and ideas they draw from Internet contents. Both myths will be examined in this book. Other reference sources, such as *Bartleby* <www.bartleby.com> may bundle numerous reference sources together and offer these free of charge. *Bartleby* features *Columbia Encyclopedia*, *American Heritage Dictionary*, *Roget's II: The New Thesaurus*, *Columbia World of Quotations*, *Bartlett's Familiar Quotations*, *King James Bible*, *Oxford Shakespeare*, *Gray's Anatomy*, *Strunk's Elements of Style*, *World Factbooks*, and *Columbia Gazetteer*. In order to access reference sources, use library catalogs, described next.

- **Library catalogs** will show which books and other book-like publications are locally available in your own library by and about Benjamin Franklin. As a result of your library search, benjamin franklin, you will see a list of short titles displayed on a computer screen for books that match your search, benjamin franklin. In order to locate some of these publications, select desired titles one at a time. Each selected title will display a detailed cataloging record for the corresponding book including the author's name, full title, publication date, physical description, and call number. It is important to write down call numbers for all books you wish to read or borrow from your library. Some books may not be available to you in your local library; however, knowing important data such as title and author, will help your librarian borrow these publications from other libraries through a service known as interlibrary loan. Chapter 6 will give more details on how to find books by means of using library catalogs. Most of today's library catalogs are on the Web, including your own school or college library catalog. So, it is convenient to search any library holdings from your home, work place, or dorm; you do not have to go to the library to search or browse library collections. More details are described next, in the section on remote library catalogs.

- **Remote library catalogs** will show records representing writings by and about Benjamin Franklin that are located remotely—away from your school library. If you search the University of California's online library catalog <melvyl.cdlib.org>, you will see records that describe documents about Franklin's views on the education of youth in Pennsylvania, and his essays on government, ethics, and economy. These documents may be stored in different University of California campus libraries. In order to physically locate some of these documents, you would have to search the individual libraries that own some of the writing that are related to Benjamin Franklin. WorldCat <www.worldcat.org> is the Online Computer Library Center's Union Catalog that offers access to the world's information in numerous languages, formats, and media.

- **Online databases** are defined as collections of electronic entries searchable in a variety of ways and organized for easy and efficient retrieval. Examples of databases include ProQuest, EBSCOhost, InfoTrac, and JSTOR. Contents may be searchable by author, title, or subject; the result will be articles published in magazines, journals, or newspapers. ARTstor offers access to online images from numerous collections. All these databases may be available by subscription from your libraries. Some printed magazine titles might be available in your own library. Others can be obtained through interlibrary loan. More on how to look up articles is in Chapter 8.

- **Archives** typically include primary documents such as personal letters and correspondence, diaries, period costumes, and other cultural objects that were a part of a person or an organization. An example is Franklin's Archive in Philadelphia, which is available on the Web. It will take you through a virtual multimedia gallery of his scientific experiments in electricity and other achievements in politics, philosophy, printing, and music writing. You will see his portraits and manuscripts at <sln.fi.edu/franklin/rotten.html>. Another is the Online Archive of California at <www.oac.cdlib.org>. It brings together tens of thousands of primary sources (defined as records created by participants in the event being studied) from historical societies, museums, and archives. Glancing through a list of Finding Aids, you will get a sense of a wide variety of types of digital materials available to us. You will discover many more Web resources in Chapter 7. You will also learn that not everything that is on the Web is of equally high quality. You will learn how to identify and select good sites. See Appendix D, "Getting Started with Primary Sources."

These four types of retrieval systems: reference sources; library catalogs; online databases of magazine, journal, and newspaper articles; and archival collections, are organized and searched differently. We suggest that you start your search with encyclopedias and the library catalog. These will point you to books and other reference sources that are closest to you.

To *ask* a good question means to express an information need as broad or as specific as the need may be. For example, if you wanted to find books on the origins or causes of the American Revolution, your question should not be at the level of U.S. politics and government in general or about the state of Massachusetts in particular. The question might incorporate phrases or keywords such as united states revolution causes; in fact, the official subject heading is United States—Revolution, 1775-1783—Causes.

Psychologists, physicians, engineers, and other professionals have each developed their own language to communicate their ideas effectively. You will be a better user of library research tools if you are comfortable with terms such as reference sources and the differences among a variety of sources, classification schemes, and library catalogs. Other library-related activities include interlibrary loan, access, and borrowing policies. These concepts, along with those pertaining to evaluating, citing, and summarizing (see Chapter 9, Appendix N), finding good search terms (see Chapter 2), and constructing search strategies (see Chapter 3) are the foundation of knowing how to access, locate, interpret, and evaluate sources. *The end result is to be able to think critically about contents, draw conclusions based on evidence, try to generate new knowledge, and share that knowledge ethically and productively.* Especially important are six **Think Guides**, located in the back of the corresponding chapters and 17 **Appendices** in the back of this book.

Location of informal information sources (unpublished material)

It is useful to consider the communication process in the broader context of locating information (see Figure 1.2). In such a setting, the simplest communication model, referred to as Model 1, operates under the general assumption that there is a sender who initiates a message (CREATOR), and a receiver of that message (USER).

Model 1 assumes that messages exchanged between the creator and the user are of short duration, informal in nature, and interactive regardless of the place and their content. Messages are exchanged electronically, face-to-face, by phone, and fax. Students and instructors transfer their files remotely, and participate in debates from virtual classrooms. In each of these settings people can modify their behavior and messages instantly to account for specific age groups, language skills, literacy levels, and cultural differences. There is no imposed system of organization on the informal information sources other than their inner file organization.

Creator ⟷ User

Internal Communication
- short message
- interaction between creator and user

Examples:
- face-to-face debate
- phone/fax messages
- electronic mail (e-mail, blogs, podcasts)
- public speaking

Figure 1.2: Communication—Model 1

Location of formal information sources (published material)

Figure 1.3 represents a more complex level of communication between the creator and the user. As messages become longer, they get published in a variety of formats, such as books, magazine articles, music albums, and software programs. This recorded knowledge is stored in bookstores and libraries; it is arranged in various ways.

Since the famed Alexandria Library of Ancient Egypt, people have worked hard to organize recorded knowledge for different purposes. On one side of the spectrum is the example of a personal library where documents may be organized by size, by most recently acquired material, and by quality—a stack of good books. A bookstore organizes its publications, classifying them by fiction, nonfiction, best sellers, biographies, cookbooks, and travel. Other clearinghouses may use multiple copies of titles: one copy under fiction, another as a best seller, and so on. While these different schemes may suffice in small collections, they are often inadequate for large collections. So, there is an additional layer of organization—the library catalog, as illustrated in Model 3.

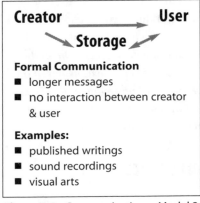

Figure 1.3: Communication—Model 2

Location of information via "filters":
Finding a needle in a haystack

Model 3 has an additional layer between the creator and the user (see Figure 1.4). While readers can go directly to a library or bookstore and browse its material, it may be faster and more efficient to first search a catalog—an example of a filter between documents and users. Other filtering mechanisms include bibliographies, such as *Books in Print*, or items on the Internet <www.amazon.com> and online databases, such as ProQuest <proquest.umi.com> or JSTOR <www.jstor.org>. Library catalogs are designed to rapidly lead you to desired items in a collection.

This model assumes that there is a fairly large collection of material and that the user is familiar with library organization. Library catalogs have added unique features to the library organization in the following two ways:

1. A catalog has an additional layer between the author or creator and the user. It allows library items to be arranged according to a classification scheme, not sequentially, in the order in which items arrive at the library, or according to broad topics (e.g., Yahoo!'s broad groups such as cars, finance, games, music, sports, TV, and yellow pages).

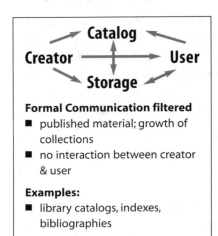

Figure 1.4: Communication—Model 3

2. Each library item is identified, described, classified, and given a call number which uniquely represents that item. Call numbers are independent of a specific shelf location; they are only linked to the item.

How people look up information:
From hunter-gatherer to sophisticated user

User ――――――→ Creator

Model 1: Hunter-Gatherer
- picking up bits of information from areas which are most likely to give desired results

Examples:
- browsing and exploring through bookstores, libraries, and personal files

Figure 1.5: Seeking behavior—Model 1

The most common way of looking up information is random, exploratory, and not planned out in advance (see Figure 1.5). Therefore, you are "hunting and gathering" bits of information as you go along.

The setting may be a bookstore, personal files, or your library. This informal information seeking style may lead to surprising discoveries. The process of exploration, while time consuming, is an important learning experience.

The next stage of information seeking is more directed than the one of the Hunter/Gatherer. Scanning presumes a certain organizational structure in place (see Figure 1.6).

User ――――――→ Creator
Titles

Model 2: Early thinker
- a more directed and systematic search to determine the utility of most relevant titles

Examples:
- scanning titles of the most promising publishers and/or authors
- skimming over content pages of books and magazines

Figure 1.6: Seeking behavior—Model 2

Search, for example, for titles published by W. W. Norton on the Colonial period, 1600-1775. Chances are that if you are a fairly sophisticated searcher, you will use retrieval filters, including library catalogs and other databases, in order to locate desired materials on your topic.

The following section will show a road map to locating sources.

Search strategy road map

The strategy assumes that the student is an *inexperienced* library searcher. Let's assume that she is a tourist in a town never visited before. Chances are that a map of that town would help demystify road patterns and streets, give some orientation, point to interesting places, and give an overall sense of the town. To use this analogy in a library setting, we show a road map to information sources (see Figure 1.7).

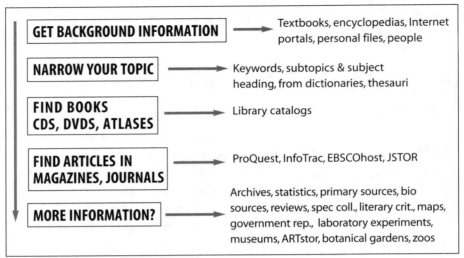

Figure 1.7: Road map to sources

Start off by using encyclopedias to get the big picture. Examples are *World Book Encyclopedia* and *Encyclopedia Britannica.* The electronic version is at <school.eb.com> (for details see Chapter 4). Search library catalogs by author/title or topics. A way to look up books by what they are about is to use keywords; this will give you a list of entries that describe books in your local library. Look at the fields called subject headings in the retrieved entries; these are "official" subjects assigned to the books by librarians. If the books look relevant, use these subject headings to find more books, CDs, and DVDs on that topic (see Chapter 2). We will learn how to use these words to search the library catalog and find books in your own library (Chapters 3, 6). To access magazine and newspaper articles, search databases such as ProQuest and JSTOR (Chapter 8). Internet and biographical/literary information (Chapters 7, 5) will offer complementary perspectives to your reports. Finally, we will show how to cite and evaluate any or all of these sources before you incorporate them into your written or oral reports (Chapters 7, 9).

Types of questions

Now that you are in the library with a map, chances are that you have a series of questions to clarify. This is a good starting point in library research. Figure 1.8 gives examples of different types of questions you might have.

One class of questions, "kind of information," will lead you to the appropriate type of reference source. For example, in the **book review** example, you will find reviews in newspapers (e.g., *Los Angeles Times, New York Times, New York Review of Books* at <www.nybooks.com>. In larger libraries, and especially college libraries, you will want to find excerpts from reviewing sources in one place. Use the *Book Review Digest* <www.hwwilson.com/brdig.htm> and look first under the author's name in the author index.

What kind of information? Examples:
- Book (performance, movie) reviews
- Addresses of schools, movie theaters, political representatives
- Books on groundwater pollution; poems about friendship
- Portrait of an artist (e.g., Andy Warhol)

How much information? Examples:
- An overview article about Roe v. Wade
- Best or most recent books on American short story writers

What is the purpose of required information? Examples:
- Getting started for a project in AP or honor science class
- Collecting information for a graduate student or history scholar

---

Figure 1.8: Types of questions to ask

The other class of questions, "how much information," is equally important. For an overview article about Roe v. Wade, a seventh grade student might be happy with an encyclopedia article (e.g., from *World Book Encyclopedia*) and books. Bibliographies, primary sources, or magazine articles on the subject might be more appropriate for a 12th grade student or college freshman.

Finally, consider the purpose of the inquiry and a given set of evaluation criteria, typically assigned by the instructor, that will focus the searching process.

Characteristics of reference sources

Figure 1.9 outlines various categories of reference sources based on five characteristics: type, time, format, medium, and detail. We can use these characteristics in selecting the ideal reference source.

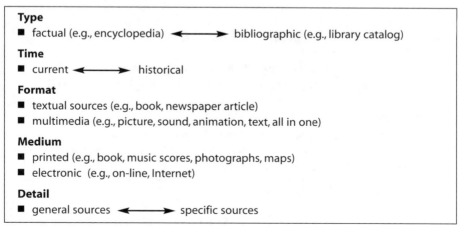

Figure 1.9: Characteristics of reference sources

Each of these five categories is described and illustrated shortly. As Figure 1.9 shows, by type of reference sources, you can select between factual sources, such as dictionaries, encyclopedias, and almanacs, and bibliographic sources, such as library catalogs and bibliographies (TYPE). In addition, some reference sources will give you current events, while others will include historical perspective only (TIME). Some sources will be mainly text-oriented, while others will contain graphics (FORMAT). While some sources are printed, others will include sound, animation, and other interactive features (MEDIUM). Finally, some sources will be simpler to use than others that have more detail and information (DETAIL).

Types of reference sources

There are two main types of reference sources (see Figure 1.10):

- **Factual sources** typically provide facts, such as the meaning of a word, the telephone number of your local pharmacy, a street map, a description of an actor's works, a baseball legend, a human rights activist. Examples of factual sources are dictionaries, directories, almanacs, handbooks, and yearbooks. Some dictionaries and encyclopedias offer brief references. For example, many articles in *The New Grove Dictionary of Music and Musicians* contain bibliographies for further reading. The same is true for many in depth encyclopedias, such as *World Book Encyclopedia* and *Encyclopedia Britannica*.

- **Bibliographic sources,** on the other hand, provide bibliographic references or citations to books and articles. They guide you to materials about your topic. Library catalogs identify and describe the library's items by means of giving the author's name, title, publisher, and date. Online magazine databases describe individual articles that appear in magazines and newspapers. Examples are ProQuest at: <proquest.umi.com> and JSTOR at <www.jstor.org> (Figure 1.10).

Factual sources
- use dictionaries—to find information about word meaning, origin, synonyms, spelling, pronunciation, usage
- use directories—to find addresses of people, schools, theaters
- use encyclopedias—for general information about a topic, person, an event, or a place

Bibliographic sources
- use library catalogs—to find books about a topic, person, or place
- use online magazine databases—ProQuest—to find articles in newspapers and magazines about people, topics, events, places

---

Figure 1.10: Types of reference sources

At the heart of all bibliographic sources is the bibliographic record. The example in Figure 1.11 is typical of bibliographic records in library catalogs. The record gives the author's name (Bruno Latour), title (Laboratory life), publication date (1986), as well as subject matter (Biology—Research; and Biology—Methodology).

Author:	Latour, Bruno
Title:	Laboratory life : the construction of scientific facts / Bruno Latour, Steve Woolgar ; introduction by Jonas Salk ; with a new postscript and index by the authors.
Published:	Princeton, N.J. Princeton University Press, c1986.
Description:	294 p. : ill. ; 22 cm.
Subjects:	Biology--Research. Biology--Methodology.

Figure 1.11: Bibliographic record

You also know the number of pages that the book contains, if it is illustrated, and its size. Note that the introduction is written by Jonas Salk—himself a key figure in biological research. An important feature of this book is an index that was created by the authors themselves.

Time of sources

Time as a characteristic of information sources is important and will be used (see Figure 1.12):

1. To limit search to a desired time: the most recent articles on civil rights; current research on DNA; to find [digital] primary source images from the civil rights movement from the periods and places the events actually happened.

2. To ask a specific question, such as "how are anxiety disorders currently treated?"

Today's movies and plays?
- possible answers: today's newspaper, web pages, blogs

General Election (November 7, 2008)
- possible answers: newspaper articles, weekly popular magazines, the Web

The Iraq War (2003 invasion)
- magazine articles, almanacs, books

Figure 1.12: Time as a characteristic of reference sources

Chances are that you will need to read current materials only. So if your search matches hundreds of items on civil rights, you might want to limit to a particular year. By selecting a specific time period, your search result will be more focused.

For current information that has not been printed in magazine articles, chances are that you will find plenty in the news and on the Internet—here's how:

where PAPERNAME is replaced by the actual title of a newspaper:

www.nytimes.com/

www.infoworld.com/

www.elpais.es/

If you are prepared to wait for journal articles, books, and encyclopedia articles to be published, which takes time, chances are that the writing will be less current but well researched and peer-reviewed by the scholarly community. You will also have a wider choice of sources to select from. So, the further you are removed from a specific date, the more sources will be available to you. Published sources in established journals will be more scholarly in nature, will be peer-reviewed, will have bibliographies, and should be more reliable and valid. This process is time-consuming and may take up to one year or more to complete. This means that you may have to wait longer for a book to be published than for a newspaper article to be printed. The price for this quality is time.

Format of sources

Information may be represented in many different formats, such as books, atlases, photographs, manuscripts, and other formats (see Figure 1.13). Include in your papers information from a variety of available formats.

Book-like publications
- books, anthologies, and albums (paper and digital format)

Cartographic publications
- maps, aerial photographs, atlases (paper and digital)

Sound recordings
- compact discs, MP3

Pictures and photographs
- still images, movies, posters, cartoons and illustrations (paper and digital)

Multimedia
- graphics, animation, audio, text, all in one document (e.g., Internet)

Figure 1.13: Format as a characteristic of reference sources

Let's say you write an illustrated children's book. The content is represented in the form of a book. A TV producer comes along and decides that the content of that book would be ideal for her new TV educational series. She uses text, animation, and audio, based on the content of your book. Your ideas are being transformed from the BOOK form to the MOVING PICTURE form.

Do not limit yourself to books, or any other single format. Use a wide range of available resources regardless of format or medium.

Same content— different media

Just about any reference source can appear in a variety of media—another characteristic of information sources. The same content may be packaged as a printed book, as a computer database, and on the Internet (see Figure 1.13).

EXERCISE 1.1: Printed versus Internet version of the same content

In order to get a feel for some of the differences between printed and electronic media, try using the following source: *Encyclopedia Britannica* <http://school.eb.com> and its multivolume printed version. Search for information on **biomes**. Compare and contrast these two versions and answer the following questions:

1. Which of the two versions (printed, Web) was easier for you to use and why?

2. Which version was faster to find the desired information?

3. Which version of the *Encyclopedia Britannica* was more interesting to use; explain why?

4. Comment on the general structure, hyperlinks, and the use of navigational buttons.

5. Does the Web page lead you to further readings and other useful links?

Level of detail

Level of detail is another characteristic of information sources. By "level of detail," we mean that not all sources will be of equal specificity, length, and scope. An article in *World Book Encyclopedia* on Nat Turner may give you just enough information to get you started in the right direction. Another source might give you more detail, more facts, and more leads to find further readings on your own, and so forth.

If you are exploring an area of **human rights**, the following general sources may be helpful as a starting point in your library search:

1. **Encyclopedias and handbooks:** *World Book Encyclopedia*; *Encyclopedia Britannica*; more specific titles will be found in larger libraries; an example is *Encyclopedia of Human Rights*.

2. **Library catalogs:** check library catalogs for books on civil rights. Trace specific political figures who significantly contributed to the civil rights movement in the 1960s.

3. **Online magazine databases:** ProQuest, EBSCOhost, and JSTOR. More specific sources will be mentioned in Chapter 7.

4. **Archival sources:** Library of Congress sites <www.loc.gov> offer a large and well-organized collection of digital primary sources in different formats.

5. **Search engines and portals:** Google <www.google.com> and Librarians' Internet Index <lii.org>.

Asking a good question or shaping a topic for your term-paper

Let us say your teacher has given you the opportunity to choose a topic that interests you and then to write a paper on it. The best advice is to choose something that is intriguing and that you want to learn more about. The following cookbook technique will work in most cases. Many of the points we have discussed thus far may also be applied to defining a paper topic.

- Start with a general topic: health, global change, music, Benjamin Franklin.

- Apply any of the information characteristics on the general topic: another topic, time, a particular publication form, or location.

Example: Health

There are many documents written on various aspects of health. You need to narrow down this general topic. Here is how:

(a) Add a subtopic (example: health and fitness among teenagers)
(b) Limit to a specific geographic area (example: United States)
(c) Limit to publication formats (example: magazine articles, almanacs, GoogleScholar at <scholar.google.com>, RSS feeds)
(d) Focus results to time period or language (example: last 10 years in English)
(e) Your working topic might be as follows:

Identify sources published within last 10 years that discuss trends of health and fitness among teenagers in the United States.

Your final topic selection will furthermore depend on the purpose of the assigned project (e.g., essay, presentation, or proposal) and evaluation criteria by your instructor to achieve a certain score.

To get some practice, use the template given below. The template is divided into three parts. The first part is reserved for a general topic. The second part contains some of the characteristics that we introduced earlier. In the third part, include the specific title for your term paper.

Part 1. Your general topic: (example: Thomas S. Hutchinson; you may substitute any other historical figure, such as Jane Addams, Ida B. Wells-Barnett, Elizabeth Cady Stanton)

Part 2. Narrow down your general topic by using any or all of the following characteristics:
(a) Subtopic (example: U.S. politics and government up to 1775— Colonial period)
(b) Geographic area (example: Massachusetts)
(c) Publication format (example: books, portraits)
(d) Time and language, when appropriate (example: most recent English documents)
(e) Medium (example: printed, selected Internet sources)

Part 3. Your focused topic: English language books that include illustrations published recently on the impact Thomas Hutchinson had on the causes of American Revolution; information in printed sources is preferred.

You can work out several examples using this template. Select topics from history, sciences, the arts, and other subject matters. See **Think Guide #1** at the end of this chapter for more examples on how to narrow down a topic. Appendices E through G give examples for possible projects in the sciences (Appendix E), arts (Appendix F), and social sciences (Appendix G).

What you have learned

In Chapter 1 we learned that there is a wide variety of sources that you can explore and use in your work. They differ by type, time, format, medium, and level of detail. Different sources are organized differently. They are searched differently, too. The chapter presented a road map (Figure 1.7) and suggests a sequence of sources that you might find useful in your research. You do not have to always start with encyclopedias, but these sources are helpful starting points, especially if you are exploring a topic. This chapter also introduced some basic terms and concepts that you will find throughout this book.

You learned that asking a good question and focusing on your term paper is important. Several examples illustrate how a fairly general topic can be narrowed down so that it is manageable in your research effort. In addition, Think Guide #1 at the end of this chapter provides space for you to practice and master this research skill.

Planning library research early on is important for thorough and efficient work. Here, you may use a well-known analogy. If you want to watch an important sporting event, you need to make plans well in advance. Make sure that you are free that day, buy tickets, and coordinate with your friends. Library research takes time, and planning is critical.

Now you can think about your term papers the way most experts do. They break down their research activity into smaller parts, design an overall plan, ask questions:

- Which types of sources are the first best sources?
- Do I have to visit other libraries (virtually or physically)?
- If the library borrows an item from another library through an interlibrary loan service, how much time will it take before I actually get that item?

Finally, you gather information. You will most likely modify your initial interest because, in the process, you learned and asked good questions. You might start off your research journey with a broad heading, such as "beat generation." Upon refining the topic, you learn more about the movement as presented by specific writers and their works. Finally, you decide to write about Jack Kerouac's *On the Road*. Researching is not a linear process; it goes through many loops, spirals, dips, and uneven learning curves. Most of the time, however, library research and exploration are rewarding activities.

Think Guide 1 Topic Narrowing Exercise

Introduction to the teachers and media specialists: The topic-narrowing guide has two parts. We will first show a worked out example; then you will find a blank form so that you can use it with your students. This form is the extension of the section "Asking a good question or shaping a topic for your term paper" in Chapter 1. It can work well both for imposed questions and student-generated questions. Typically, students will work on teacher assigned projects.

Getting started right. Students will be asked to write a paper, present their work in class, prepare some type of visual (poster, chart, brochure, model, diorama), or work on an assignment on a given topic. The topic here is taken broadly, to include people, places, events, processes, timelines, materials, and concepts. Students will approach their assignments differently, depending on their familiarity with the topic, their grade level, the subject matter, and the purpose of the project.

A narrowing down exercise requires a mix of cognitive demands on students, including collaboration in small teams, communication skills, learning new concepts, connecting to known concepts, problem solving techniques, and so forth.

What follows is a general Think Guide that will help students focus or narrow down their topic.

EXAMPLE: Topic narrowing described and annotated

Larger topics (to Roman Empire): ancient civilizations ➔ civilizations ➔ history/art/classics

This means that if you searched under "ancient civilizations," your books and other publications may be on any known civilization: Egypt, China, Greece, Rome, Persia, and not just on the Roman Empire.

Assigned topic
"Roman Empire"

Also known as ancient Rome, Latin civilization (you may also use these words to search material on the Roman Empire).

Smaller topics (to Roman Empire): students may use any of the following words to narrow down their general topic of Roman Empire, such as Roman laws, Roman gods. The list below is not arranged in any particular order. Ask the students to cluster similar words together and show, if possible, how various words and clusters are related to one another.

---

army; vessels, navy; sieges and campaigns
emperors; specific emperors (Caesar, Augustus); citizens
temples, baths, arches, aqueducts; the Forum; gardens
gods; religion
laws
literature; the arts; architecture; cities (Pompeii, Herculaneum)
administration; colonies
slavery; types of gladiators; freedman
education
family; children, women, costumes; homes; meal
courtship, marriage
sickness, healing, medicine
death; excavation

---

time: 510 B.C.–476 A.D.

place: Rome, Italy, Mediterranean

types of sources: printed, electronic, Web-based encyclopedias, books, pictures, maps

Exercise: Topic narrowing

Larger topics (than assigned):

Assigned topic

Also known as:

Smaller topics (to assigned topic):

time:

place:

types of sources:

CHAPTER

2

Finding Search Words

In this chapter, you will learn how:

- To search library collections by using search words (keywords, subject headings)
- To differentiate between subject headings and keywords
- To use the power of a classification system (such as Dewey Decimal Classification) and to get familiar with user-created taxonomies and a semantic web

This chapter focuses on important tools that will help you in searching materials by what they are about. In other words, we want to spend some time on the many ways we can search library material by subject. For extensive and "how-to-do-it" illustrations and tips, see **Think Guide 2**, **Finding Search Words**, at the end of this chapter as well as Appendices H1 and H2.

How do we access publications?

There are two main approaches to searching library publications: by knowing the name of an author (creator) or title (also known as "known-item search"); and by exploring the subject matter of a desired publication ("subject search"). This chapter will show you how to search books, DVDs, CDs, maps, and other publications according to their subject matter. As experts say, the less you know about a topic you are hoping to find material about, the harder it is to express what you are really trying to find in any collection, physical or virtual. For a moment, we will assume that we *know* the subject matter we are interested in and that these subject words will be helpful to us to find library materials.

Suppose that the book in your hands has the following information: the author is Mark Twain; the title is *Adventures of Huckleberry Finn*; other items of interest might be that the book was published in 1996 by Random House in New York. Using some of these data, how would you search the book to find out if there is another copy somewhere in your library? You are probably guessing correctly. You would search by the author's name, *mark twain*, and the title of the publication, *adventures of huckleberry finn*. This is why this type of search is called a known-item search. As a result of your search, you would see a library catalog entry like the one in Figure 2.1.

Author: Twain, Mark, 1835-1910.
Title: Adventures of Huckleberry Finn / Mark Twain ; introduction by Justin Kaplan ; foreword and addendum by Victor Doyno.
Edition: 1st ed.
Published: New York : Random House, c1996.
Description: xxviii, 418 p. : ill. ; 25 cm.
Subject(s):   Finn, Huckleberry (Fictitious character)--Fiction.
            Boys--Travel--Mississippi River--Fiction.
            Boys--Missouri--Fiction.

Call number: FIC TWA 1996

Figure 2.1: Cataloging entry

However, if you did not know either the name of the author or the title of the book, you would probably try to search by subject. If you were to search this book by subject, how would you do it? Surely, from the example above, you might just look at the subject headings, labeled "Subject(s)," that are assigned to the book to find if the library has more books on the same or similar topics. Depending on how much you know about Twain's *Adventures*, you could search by means of the following headings:

Authors, American--19th century.
Authors, American--19th century--Biography.
Boys--Travel--Mississippi River--Fiction.
Boys--Missouri--Fiction.
Finn, Huckleberry (Fictitious character)--Fiction.
Mississippi River--Description and travel.
Mississippi River--Fiction.
Mississippi River Valley--Social life and customs.
Twain, Mark, 1835-1910--Journeys--Mississippi River Valley.

Figure 2.2: Library of Congress Subject Headings (LCSH)

To help you "discover" official subject headings that are assigned by catalogers to describe what the materials in their collections are about, there are several widely used techniques; to get you started, search by using your own keywords, identify potentially relevant books from that search, and look at the subject headings in the displayed entries (see Figures 2.1, 2.2, 2.3). Use these subject headings, also known as Library of Congress Subject Headings (LCSH) to find more books and other materials on the same or similar topics.

Another technique is to search subject headings online on the Web at <authorities.loc.gov>. In a dialog box, type in your keyword and select "Subject Authorities Headings." For example, if your keyword was global warming, the list will produce other terms and phrases that you may have not been aware of before. My quick search of that phrase produced the following list of subheadings that make "global warming" more specific:

global warming
global warming decision making moral and ethical aspects
global warming environmental aspects
global warming environmental aspects case studies
global warming environmental aspects (subdivided geographically)
global warming fiction
global warming government policy (subdivided geographically)
global warming health aspects
global warming history
global warming law and legislation (subdivided geographically)
global warming prevention
global warming public opinion
global warming research
global warming statistical methods

Figure 2.3: Partial list of subject headings (LCSH) related to global warming

Nowadays, library catalogs on the Web make it easy to discover official subject headings via the keyword approach. Simply use a browse button (rather than search) on a single keyword or a two-word phrase; you will see a list of hyperlinked subject headings that are related to the keywords you typed in. Next to each hyperlinked subject heading, you will notice a number of records associated with the respective hyperlinked subject headings. By pointing your browser on the posted number, you will see individual records of resources in your collection that have been assigned the selected subject headings.

Yet, my own preferred way of finding subject headings is to look them up in the printed subject headings (LCSH). As a result, you will be displayed relationships between and among subject headings that are not given in the online lists. For example, some terms are preferred, some are synonymous; yet others are more specific than the main heading, related to the main heading, such as "greenhouse effect, atmospheric," or broader to global warming, such as "global temperature changes." All these relationships are identified in printed editions of Library of Congress Subject Headings. For demonstration purposes, this chapter demonstrates displays on a variety of subjects. A small portion of such a display, on the topic of architecture, is given in Figure 2.4, below:

Architecture (May be Subdivided Geographically)
    Used For (UF) Building design
    Broader Term (BT) Art
    Narrower Terms (NT), e.g., arches to water and architecture
Architecture--Aesthetics
Architecture--Conservation and restoration
Architecture--17th-18th century
Architecture--20th century--Design and plans
Architecture--20th century--United States
Architecture--Aegean Islands (Greece and Turkey)
Architecture, American--New England
Architecture, Ancient--Jordan-Petra (Extinct city)
Architecture and climate--California--San Francisco
Architecture and energy conservation
Architecture and youth

Figure 2.4: A portion of LCSH on the subject of architecture

Now that you have discovered various subject headings on the topic architecture, you can use those to find books and other materials on specific aspects of architecture, architecture in different countries, and across different periods. For example, to find publications about architecture and youth, you would use the official subject heading architecture and youth. The result of your search would be a list with bibliographic descriptions of books on that topic, "architecture and youth."

An example is annotated in Figure 2.5. The added data fields are put in brackets, such as the author's name (Herb Childress), the title ("*Landscapes of betrayal* ..."), publication data (the book was published by the State University New York Press, Albany in 2000), physical description, series information, subject headings, location of that book in a library, call number, and the availability status of that book. All this information will help you decide whether to actually locate that edition of the work in library stacks. For example, the following edition is illustrated, it has introductory pages (indicated in Roman "xx"), and it is a part of the series "in environmental and architectural phenomenology." This means that there are other titles in the same series that you might want to explore.

[Author]: Childress, Herb, 1958-
[Title]: Landscapes of betrayal, landscapes of joy : Curtisville in the lives of its teenagers.
[Publication data]: Albany : State University of New York Press, c2000.
[Physical description of the book]: xx, 351 p. : ill. ; 23 cm.
[The book is part of a series]: SUNY series in environmental and architectural phenomenology.
[This book is about]:
Teenagers--California--Social conditions--Case studies.
Adolescent psychology--California--Case studies.
Spatial behavior--California--Case studies.
Teenagers and the environment--California--Case studies.
Architecture and youth--California--Case studies.
Location: YRL; Call Number: HQ796 .C458237 2000.   Status: Not Checked Out

Figure 2.5: An example of annotated cataloging entry

The Library of Congress Subject Headings is a general list of headings for all topics arranged in a single alphabetical order. In addition, there are specialized vocabularies, and many are now available on the Web as well. An example is Getty's *Art & Architecture Thesaurus* at <www.getty.edu/research/conducting_research/vocabularies/aat/>. You may want to search for words and phrases on any art and architecture object or concept (e.g., gardens; impressionism). Getty's other vocabularies are of geographic names at <www.getty.edu/research/conducting_research/vocabularies/tgn/> and of artists' names at <www.getty.edu/research/conducting_research/vocabularies/ulan/>.

Yet another vocabulary is useful for searching health related topics <www.ncbi.nlm.nih.gov>.

Getting started: How to be in a driver's seat throughout your research journey

Referring to Figure 2.3, if you were to search books on "global warming," which among the following phrases would you select?

Some of the questions you might ask are: Where do I find these words and phrases? Do I need to use all of them in searching publications? Which ones are the most useful? Do I use plural or singular? In which order do I type the multiword phrases? These are all good questions because, whenever you search computer catalogs for books, you will be searching with words and phrases. Recall our road map chart from Chapter 1 (Figure 1.7). You will notice that subject headings are used to find accurate and complete search words under which to look up items in library catalogs.

Look up the following headings in LCSH: Halloween; Boston Tea Party; Boston Colonial period; speeches; heavy metal; energy; oxygen; Aztec civilization; Nicaragua—Social conditions.

We summarize here what you may have already discovered on your own: finding LCSH in your quest for materials on global warming or architecture.

We can use LCSH as a dictionary that gives you words, synonyms, and definitions. LCSH may be thought of as a navigational tool that shows the types of relationships that exist between and among subject headings. If your search produced only a few documents, you could expand your search by using "broader terms" (BT) and "related terms" (RT). For example, in the example on architecture, the broader terms may be architectural design, design, art, and buildings.

To give you more time to practice, consider the following excerpt from LCSH on the topic of COOKERY. In Figure 2.6, the instruction in the parentheses, "May Subd Geog," means that you can search material on, for example, cookery in various geographical locations (e.g., Brazil, Japan, Spain).

EXERCISE 2.1: Questions related to LCSH

Using the LCSH example on the next page, please answer the following questions:

(a) Looking at the cookery headings in Figure 2.6, can you search for books on fat-free diets?

Yes ☐   No ☐

(b) If not, what would be an appropriate subject heading to search under?

(c) Still referring to Figure 2.6, can you search for publications under Cookery, Cook Islands?

Yes ☐   No ☐

(d) Can you recommend to your friend a correct phrase to look up for books on California style, American cookery?

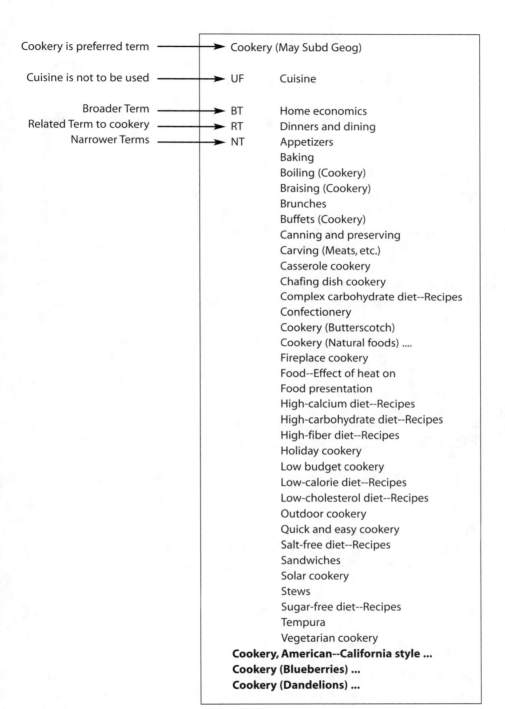

Cookery is preferred term →	Cookery (May Subd Geog)	
Cuisine is not to be used →	UF	Cuisine
Broader Term →	BT	Home economics
Related Term to cookery →	RT	Dinners and dining
Narrower Terms →	NT	Appetizers
		Baking
		Boiling (Cookery)
		Braising (Cookery)
		Brunches
		Buffets (Cookery)
		Canning and preserving
		Carving (Meats, etc.)
		Casserole cookery
		Chafing dish cookery
		Complex carbohydrate diet--Recipes
		Confectionery
		Cookery (Butterscotch)
		Cookery (Natural foods) ....
		Fireplace cookery
		Food--Effect of heat on
		Food presentation
		High-calcium diet--Recipes
		High-carbohydrate diet--Recipes
		High-fiber diet--Recipes
		Holiday cookery
		Low budget cookery
		Low-calorie diet--Recipes
		Low-cholesterol diet--Recipes
		Outdoor cookery
		Quick and easy cookery
		Salt-free diet--Recipes
		Sandwiches
		Solar cookery
		Stews
		Sugar-free diet--Recipes
		Tempura
		Vegetarian cookery

Cookery, American--California style ...
Cookery (Blueberries) ...
Cookery (Dandelions) ...

Figure 2.6: Excerpt from LCSH on "cookery"

To summarize, LCSH is designed to:

1. Control terms and phrases that are spelled the same but may have different meanings, also known as homonyms. Some examples are:

   MERCURY - may mean heavy metal, planet, goddess
   HEAVY METALS - toxic metals such as arsenic, nickel, and lead; rock group
   PITCH - like in aeronautics, in music, baseball
   PLANT - from a perspective of botany, or plant as a factory
   SARA - baked products, Superfund Act

   Homonyms are controlled with a definition of a preferred term or phrase.

2. Link terms and phrases that are spelled differently but mean the same, also known as synonyms. Some examples include:

   United States, US, USA
   LABOUR see labor
   Scientific name, *see* common name—sucrose see table sugar
   Synonymous relationships are controlled with the USE and USED FOR (UF) reference notes.

3. Show a hierarchical relationship between and among terms and phrases (e.g., broader term (BT)—*buildings* is broader to *art deco buildings*; narrower term (NT)—*Cape Cod crystal* is narrower than *crystal*, and other relationships such as related terms (RT)—*birds* is related to *ornithology*).

EXERCISE 2.2: Subject headings from different perspectives

(a) For books on rock music, especially in California, which subject headings would you use?

(b) Does your library have any books on heavy metal in the context of music rather than metallurgy? Use your library catalog, and again, turn to LCSH books and look up alphabetically. Any headings that you may use in searching your library catalog?

Last word

You are probably wondering how the different elements are put together in a multi-word subject heading. These different elements are typically in the order of: Topic, Place, Time, Form. You do not have to have all of these elements in a single heading. The word "form" refers to different literary genres, such as biographies, bird's-eye views, cartoons, criticism, drama, fiction, or poetry. Music forms may include an aria, concerto, opera, sonata, or a song.

For example, the heading **Boston Massacre, 1770,** has the main topic (Boston Massacre) and date (1770).

Other ways of searching by subject

There are several indirect ways to search library material by what they are about without using subject headings. For example, once you discover that a certain author specializes in a particular topic or subtopic, you might do the **author search** to obtain his or her list of writings; display several records and look at the subject headings. Use those headings in your subsequent searches to retrieve more books on the same or similar topics. You can also extend this search technique and search the Web under the author's name.

Another way to search library material by their subject matter is by a known **series title**. For example, to obtain a broad collection of writings on various controversial subjects (e.g., gun control, euthanasia, affirmative action, homosexuals in the military, capital punishment), search under The Opposing Viewpoints. What you will retrieve will be books with different titles and on different controversial topics; however, all of these books will be within the same series title, Opposing Viewpoints.

Probably the most common way that people search is by means of keywords; the keyword approach typically gives a broad retrieval because the computer matches your words against all subject-rich words (from titles, series titles, subject headings, table of contents, notes). However, keywords are not controlled in any way. In particular,

- homonyms are not controlled (e.g., "heavy metal" may retrieve a rock group of that genre, not items on cadmium and nickel; the word "seals" may have different meanings: animals, law, numismatics)

- synonyms are not linked (e.g., material on lead may be scattered under lead, pb, toxic substances)

This is the basic difference between searching library catalogs and Internet resources. Library materials can be searched in a variety of ways; the Internet, at the moment, is mainly a keyword search. Currently, popular types of "folksonomies" or social bookmarking are used to describe, share, and discover Web sites and images. There are several widely used software services such as delicious at <http://del.icio.us/> and flickr at <www.flickr.com/>. In contrast to controlled vocabularies, like LCSH, an Internet-based social bookmarking consists of collaboratively generated tags, which are used to label Web pages and online images.

Semantic Web has been among the tools designed to put some order on piles of electronic data that are produced in massive quantities by various creators for equally varied users of information. This technique has been widely used as a powerful educational tool to demonstrate how concepts relate to other concepts and to label types of relationships between and among concepts.

Classification system

In contrast to scientific classifications (e.g., biological taxonomy), library classifications organize writings by their topics. Examples of classification systems are: Dewey Decimal Classification (DDC) and Library of Congress Classification (LCC).

The 10 main classes in Dewey Decimal Classification are:

000 (**generalities**—computer science, dictionaries & encyclopedias, museums)
100 (**philosophy & psychology**—ethics, logic)
200 (**religion**—Christianity, Islam, Judaism, Budhism)
300 (**social sciences**—politics, government, gender studies, education)
400 (**language**—language groups, linguistics, excluding literature)
500 (**natural sciences**—astronomy, physics, chemistry, biology & mathematics)
600 (**technology**—applied sciences including medicine, engineering, cooking)
700 (**the arts**—fine and decorative arts: music, cinema, visual arts, architecture)
800 (**literature & rhetoric**—literatures of different languages)
900 (**geography & history**—books on the general history of the U.S. go under 973)

To explore subdivisions of these 10 classes of the Dewey Decimal Classification, visit the Internet Public Library site at:
<en.wikipedia.org/wiki/ Dewey_Decimal_Classification#Classes>.
Also see Appendices H1 and H2.

EXERCISE 2.3: Questions related to the Dewey Decimal Classification

Using the main DDC classes, answer the following questions:

(a) Find the general area in your library where the books on the **United States presidents** are shelved. What is the general Dewey Decimal class that contains these books?

(b) Search for books on the United States history colonial period (ca. 1600-1775). Which general class is given to books on this topic? _____

Bonus point:
(c) Where would you find current music encyclopedias?

The power of call numbers

To the users of libraries, classification is an important tool that brings together in one place (collocates) books on the same or similar topics; it also facilitates browsing, which is an important exploratory technique. Each numeral and character has an important meaning. In fact, some librarians can tell you what a book is about just by looking at the call number. For example, your librarian will know that the material in the class 510 will be on the general topic of mathematics; that books in the division 516 are on geometry; and that the Euclidean geometry books will be in the 516.2 subdivision.

Because one of the purposes of a classification system is to facilitate the browsing of books and other materials in library stacks, you can use Dewey Decimal Classification (DDC) to find more useful books. Here is how. If you already found four books on your topic and need more like those that you have, try the following:

- Notice that all your books on the general history of the United States have call numbers starting with the number "973."

- Go to the library stacks; browse the area around the books that you have found useful.

- Select additional books that you consider relevant by scanning their title, table of contents, index, preface, randomly picked pages, pictures.

- Search these books in the library catalog; find the subject headings for these additional books. Use these subject headings in your subsequent searches.

What you have learned

Chapter 2 concentrated on the various approaches to subject searching. In particular, we introduced the importance of searching via keywords and subject searching, and the various ways to use browse and search library catalogs. The chapter introduced you to the concept of classification, and in particular, to the Dewey Decimal Classification System. The power of call numbers is illustrated.

This chapter has introduced the following terms and concepts. We define the main vocabulary.

Call number	Unique identification number assigned to each library item. In addition, it facilitates browsing of items on shelves. A book on Chicano rock music by David Reyes will uniquely be identified by its call number 781.66 REY.
Dewey Decimal Classification System (DDC)	DDC classifies books and book-like publications into 10 main classes (e.g., books on "music" will be grouped in class 780; general math books go under class 510). The classification groups library books on the same or similar subjects together and separates from books on unrelated subjects.

Folksonomy	A folksonomy, also known as "social tagging," or social taxonomy, is a collaboratively generated labeling of Internet contents such as Web pages, online photographs, blogs, and Web links. Examples include del.icio.us and flickr, designed for shared tagging.
Library of Congress Subject Headings (LCSH)	LCSH is a vocabulary designed to control homonyms, synonyms, and to assist you in searching for broader and narrower topics. It also suggests subject headings related to the ones you used.
Semantic Web	Emerging Web-based information retrieval techniques that are used to organize Web contents, provide access and linkages between and among disparate pieces of information on the Web in order to facilitate search, selection, and retrieval of desired information as a response to one's need. Melvil Dewey organized successfully in the context of library books.
Subject Headings	Subject headings are controlled search terms used to find accurate and complete subjects under which to look up books and other materials in library catalogs. These can be single words (e.g., Cookery) or multiword phrases (e.g., Massachusetts—History—Colonial period.—ca. 1600-1775).

For more specific books, use more specific subject headings, such as Boston Massacre, 1770, and Boston Tea Party, 1773.

Think Guide 2 Finding Search Words

Introduction to teachers and media specialists: Once the students have been assigned projects and have a general research plan, they will start to think about specific words and phrases that they will use in searching encyclopedias, library catalogs, and magazine databases. Where do they find the "right" words? Think Guide #2 is designed to save students' time and improve their skills.

The best sources for finding the "right" words are encyclopedias, textbooks, some dictionaries, and the library vocabulary that we discuss earlier in Chapter 2, **Library of Congress Subject Headings**. The rule of thumb is that the more students know about a topic they are searching on, the more successful they will be in finding the "right" vocabulary. In addition, imagination helps.

Hints that will save time and improve student's skills:

> Think of a topic that includes your topic.
> Example: your topic is BASKETBALL; the topics that include this topic are ball sports, team sports, and sports, in general. These topics are **broader** than the one you are searching on.

> Think of a topic that is:
>> A part of your topic;
>> A member of your topic;
>> That your topic is divided into;
>> That your topic consists of.
> *Example:* your topic is still basketball; the subtopic that is a part of basketball is basketball teams, players, coaches, basketball competitions, championships, strategies, etc. These topics are **narrower** or more specific than the topic you are searching on.

> Think of a variant topic (word-order) such as
>> Spelling variation;
>> Popular name;
>> Dialect of;
>> Point-of-view.
> These are **synonymous** terms. Good sources for finding the "right" words and synonyms and antonyms are the *Library of Congress Subject Headings* (an excellent source for basketball) and *Roget's Thesaurus*.

Worked out example #1: Finding search words on basketball

We will start off by giving you two examples under the heading, athletics; the topics are: **basketball**, and the **Olympic Games** 2000. The assigned topics appear in a box. Words above the box are more general topics than basketball; words and phrases below basketball are narrower. The effect will be that there will be more material on the broader topics than on the more specific ones. For example, you will find more books in your library on the general topic of SPORTS than on basketball alone, or on the NBA, LA's Lakers, Kobe, Indiana's Pacers, and so on.

The example below consists of our own words and depends on how much we know about BASKETBALL; this author's knowledge about ball games is limited, so she does not have an extensive vocabulary in this area. If you were a basketball coach or a fan, chances are your vocabulary would be more elaborate. For the purposes of comparison, compare the vocabulary below with the LCSH on basketball.

Sports   Use dictionaries to define the meaning of the word "sports." You may find different words that people use to mean sports, such as athletics, games.

Team sports   Find out which sports are called "team sports." Write down several examples of team sports; is diving a team sport (archery, swimming, water polo, tae kwon do, track-and-field)?

Basketball   Find rules, timeline, and how it started; find statistical information.
Learn about similar sports, such as volleyball, handball, soccer, water polo.

— Competitions (world, national, local); the Olympics; Special Olympics
       — Professional team competition versus college team competition
         — NBA championships
           — NBA championship 2000 (Los Angeles)
           — Lakers (LA team)
           — Phil Jackson, coach
           — Kobe Bryant, etc.

Worked out example #2: Finding search words on Olympic Games

The Olympic Games

Athletics

        Competitive Athletics

            The Olympic Games (also known as Olympics)

                Summer, Winter

                Special Olympics

The Olympic Games 2000	Sydney Harbor

Archery
Badminton
Baseball
Basketball
Boxing
Diving
Fencing
Gymnastics
Handball
Judo
Modern pentathlon
Soccer
Swimming
Table tennis
Tae kwon do
Tennis
Track-and-field
Volleyball
Water polo
Weight lifting
Wrestling

Sydney Olympic Park

Exercise: Finding the right words on your own

Think of larger topics that might include the one you are trying to understand.

Does it fall into history, geography, philosophy, civics, the sciences, the arts, many different interrelated topics (often called interdisciplinary)? If so, is there a predominant topic?

Is your topic predominantly about:

You will find it in the following sources

- **IDEAS**
  encyclopedias, books, selected Web sites
  Check for definitions, overview, biases, references

- **PEOPLE**
  encyclopedias, biographical dictionaries, books, the Web
  Check for name spelling, name variations, time, place, and contributions

- **PLACES**
  maps, atlases, the Web, encyclopedias, almanacs, books
  Check for variations in place names, sources of compilation (governments, scholarly societies)

- **UNKNOWN WORDS**
  dictionaries, encyclopedias (check for spelling, synonyms)

How much do you already know about your topic?

If nothing or little, find an article in an encyclopedia-or your textbook, and follow the road map from Chapter 1, Figure 1.7.

Think of smaller (narrower, more specific) topics that might be part of your topic. See our example of TYPES OF Olympic Games (from archery to wrestling).

- List all subtopics that might be a type of, or part of your topic

- Cluster subtopics that are similar into individual classes, like all team sports together

At first, finding the right words may seem difficult; however, with enough practice and familiarity with your topic, it becomes much easier. Remember, in the long run we're trying to make your search for information more efficient and effective.

CHAPTER

Search Strategies

In this chapter, you will learn how:

- To plan your search by using various search strategies
- To search library collections by using various subject approaches
- To use Boolean operators (i.e., AND, OR, NOT) to connect concepts and search words together
- To modify search results: (a) expand search results (if few records are retrieved), and (b) narrow down search results (if too many records are retrieved)
- To demonstrate that the introduced search strategies are universal and applied in most services (e.g., ranging from online library catalogs to search engines)

This chapter focuses on the concept of "search strategy" as it relates to searching online library catalogs, magazine and newspaper databases, or Web pages and digital collections. A search strategy is defined as an overall plan for a search problem in order to achieve a particular goal. For example, if your goal is to write a paper about sports in Rome you need to have a strategy that would help you compile a list of publications on the topic of sports in Rome. Some examples of research topics may be to describe towns and the early American settlements; to discuss the early settlers and to look at the countries they came from; to report on the various ways that historical figures such as John Hancock and Thomas Hutchinson shaped the development and growth of early American politics, government, and society; to discuss social issues in the work of 19th century and early 20th century American reformers, such as Horace Mann, Dorothea Dix, John Muir, and Margaret Sanger; to explain natural phenomena such as the greenhouse effect; or to find pen-pals from Mexico or Japan and ask them about their favorite books, sports, holidays, and classes. In order to examine and answer these questions, you will use a variety of resources such as books, maps, reference sources, cartoons, photos, magazine and newspaper articles, as well as the Internet. Regardless of the format and medium, you must cite each of these sources (see Chapter 9) and arrange them alphabetically by their authors' names or some other meaningful way. The result will be your own bibliography, an essential part of your research report or presentation. A good search strategy will produce a good bibliography, a critical piece of evidence to support your own writings and theses.

Specifically, we will focus on identifying basic concepts, linking these concepts to one another, evaluating tentative results of your searches, and modifying the strategy. You will learn to:

- Combine words using basic operators to tell the system how to perform the search (we'll cover the main three operators AND, OR, and NOT, referred to as Boolean operators).

- Construct search strategies.

- Modify your search results—you will learn how to expand if you get too little; or to limit your search, if you get too much.

Once we gather search words (see Chapter 2), we are ready to link the words with one another. There are many different ways that allow us to do so.

In addition, you will learn about various types of strategies that are available to us. Oftentimes during the search process, you will want to modify your search strategy in order to increase or decrease the number of records, or alter your search in many different ways.

Basic operators: AND

The example below is the use of the AND operator. It ANDs concept A ("toys") and concept B ("Colonial America") and creates a set of documents in the shaded area or the **intersection**, where each document must deal both with the concept "TOYS" and the concept "COLONIAL AMERICA."

If you use concept A, which covers the topic of "toys" with 200 documents, and separately, concept B "colonial america" with 100 documents, the intersection of A and B might give you 40 documents. The effect of the AND operator is that it reduces the size of the retrieved set; this can be helpful if you initially obtain too many entries.

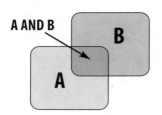

A AND B

EXERCISE 3.1: Use of the AND operator

Search your library catalog for books on **Navajo jewelry**. First type in the word Navajo in your search box; observe the number of retrieved items. Make sure that the operator is switched to the AND operator. Type in the word jewelry in a separate search box; observe the number of retrieved items. What is your conclusion? If you did the same search using one of your favorite search engines, the result would be more than 800,000 entries. You may want to add more words to AND with **Navajo jewelry**. Using Google as a search engine, this author typed in:

Navajo jewelry ---> resulted in 845,000 results (July 2007)
Navajo jewelry postage stamp ---> resulted in 66,700 items (July 2007)
"Navajo jewelry postage stamp" ---> produced a single hit, an image of a 2-cent stamp (July 2007)

You may want to explore on your own: combine "ancient civilizations" AND Swahili States (Africa). Separately, each search phrase (ancient civilization) and "Swahili States" may produce too many records. However, in the AND relationship, you will get a more precise set of records that deal with non-Western ancient civilizations, in particular with the Swahili States.

> OPTIONAL EXERCISE: Repeat this example in the Melvyl® library catalog <melvyl.cdlib.org>. Unlike your local library catalog that retrieves books that your library has, Melvyl provides access to many libraries in the state of California. Limit your search to a specific library, English language books, and to recent publications only. How many items did you find?

EXERCISE 3.2: Directed search for "team sports" in "US"

Suppose you are looking for material (e.g., books and videos) on team sports in the United States. Do the following:

1. Identify the most important concepts (example: team sports; United States)

2. Search each one separately in the library catalog (example: team sports)

3. Notice the number of results for each of these separate sets

4. Combine all sets; how many matches did you get? Example:
   team sports (AND) United States ----> number of records:

In this exercise, think of your research topic; for your topic, apply instructions a through d.

Your topic:

    (a) Identify the most important 2 concepts:

    (b) Search each concept separately:

    (c) Notice the number of results for each:

    (d) Combine sets noting the number of matches:

Basic operators: OR

This type of operator, known as the OR operator, creates the union of at least two words. (An example is the union of two words, LAWYERS or ATTORNEYS; SOCCER or FOOTBALL; SUGAR or SWEETENER; BLUBERRIES or STRAWBERRIES). The **union** creates a set of entries each of which deals with either term A (soccer) or term B (football) or both.

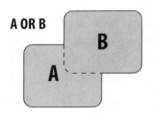

A OR B

The effect of this operator is to broaden your search, so as to give you more records. Surely, by ORing more synonymous words, your set becomes larger. If you initially get too few items, you can add more synonymous terms to make your set larger (examples might be: earrings OR necklaces; anorexia OR bulimia; Navajo OR Hopi; rugs OR quilts).

EXERCISE 3.3: Use of the OR operator

You need to find material on *early Colonies*, or on the *social conditions of Central American countries*. How would you search so that the result is as complete as possible?

(a) Which countries would you include?

(b) Which operator would you use to broaden your search?

Basic operators: NOT

The NOT operator is a powerful operator, which should be used with caution.

It allows you to eliminate all documents from your retrieval set that cover a topic that you DO NOT wish to retrieve. So, if you are not interested in documents that talk about "El Salvador," you can exclude them from your retrieval set. However, you need to be cautious because some of the documents on El Salvador

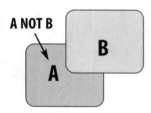

might be relevant to your general topic of "Central America." The same applies to another example: pollution. For example, if you do not exclude "air pollution," "noise pollution," and so on, you are likely to get books that contain information about these unwanted topics. So, in this context, the NOT operator is powerful yet requires caution.

EXERCISE 3.4: Use of the NOT operator

You are writing a paper on *art glass*.

(a) How would you design your search so that the retrieved books discuss only art glass and not, for example, glass animals or glass sculpture?
Your answer:

(b) You want to read material about prominent American figure Samuel Adams, and nothing on beer or breweries. What would your search look like?
Your answer:

(c) In searching photography, you find many records that mention aerial photography. Since you already know about aerial photography, you decide to eliminate this term. How do you propose to do this search?
Your answer:

Search strategy

Search strategy refers to a set of instructions that can be understood by the system you search. The search strategy specifies search words (also known as search terms) and concepts, as well as the logical relationship between and among them. You know where to find terms (see Chapter 2), and you have just learned about the three operators. We are ready to put terms and the logic together into various types of search strategies. We will start off with a "known-item" search.

- **Known-item search**—There are many reasons for using this type of search. For example, you want to verify an author's name, or to find the call number of a book recommended by your friend, or to locate it in your library, or if it is even available. In all these cases, you more or less "know" the item you want, for example, the name of the author (artist, compiler, photographer) or title, and sometimes subject; this is the reason we call it a "known-item" search.

  Another good reason to use the known-item search is to retrieve a record, and then use subject headings that are assigned to that record in order to obtain more entries. In the example of **acid rain**, you would retrieve records representing items that are about acid rain. Then you would look up subject headings that are assigned to this topic. Finally, you can use these subject headings in your subsequent searches to retrieve more of the same kinds of material. Get the call numbers for these newly retrieved records. What do they have in common? Compare their subject headings. Compare their call numbers.

- **Building block search**—This type of search strategy, the "building block" strategy, focuses on identifying "blocks" or your main concepts. This strategy is more systematic than the known-item search. Use paper and pencil to prepare in advance before you "go online." Here is how the building block strategy works:

  Step 1: Identify your main concepts ("blocks")

  Step 2: Identify terms within each concept

  Step 3: OR synonymous words within each separate block (or box)

  Step 4: AND concepts horizontally

  Step 5: Use paper and pencil before you "go online"

  Step 6: Evaluate your options

  Suppose that your research paper is on the **history of team sports** in **the New England states**. The first thing you need to do is to identify distinct blocks: history; team sports; New England states. Next you need to list synonymous terms in each block. For example, the team sports block might include baseball, volleyball, football; the New England block might include individual states such as Rhode Island, Maine, Massachusetts, etc. It will save you a lot of time if you copy the template below for each search, at least in the beginning. For examples, see **Think Guide #3** at the end of this chapter.

The basic message is that there should be a difference between the CONCEPTS and your WORDS. Concepts are used to represent important and discrete themes in your search. The concepts are ANDed across the template. WORDS are ORed within each of the concepts in the boxes below.

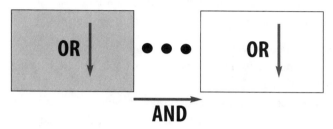

Modification: broadening and narrowing down your search

Now is a good time to look at the search results, and assess your progress so far. You have learned useful techniques, but you want to improve your searching skills. There are several techniques that will improve your search results. This section focuses on two of these techniques: broadening and narrowing your search results.

Broadening your search results. You will sometimes retrieve too few records. To get more, try the following four approaches:

- By deleting an entire search BLOCK, you will increase your search considerably; delete the least useful block, the most generic block first; with each block deleted, you will have a fewer number of AND connectors.

- By adding synonymous words within each of your blocks, you will again increase the size of your search set; add equivalent words (e.g., US, U.S.A, United States of America) and then observe the number of results.

- By adding broader words, you will see the difference in your search result (broader to time travel fiction American are terms such as time travel fiction, science fiction, novels, short stories, literature).

- Finally, you can truncate each of the concepts and words to further expand your search results. The word "truncate" means that you can sometimes search on the word root, such as law?. The symbol "?" will automatically search all words that match law or laws or lawful or lawyers. This feature depends on the source you are searching, such as the Web, online magazine database, library catalogs. Note: the search word law will rarely automatically map to attorneys.

Narrowing your search strategy. If you wish to get a smaller set of documents because you obtained too many initially, here are a few techniques to help you do so.

- Add another concept; your result will decrease. Make sure you use an appropriate operator (i.e., AND, OR NOT).

- Use as specific words as you can find. For example, search under the word opera rather than the phrase vocal music (Bali rather than Indonesia; Roe v. Wade rather than abortion; anorexia rather than eating disorders, etc.).

Further describe your main words, when possible and appropriate, with another topic, place, or specific format, such as a map, book, desired language such as English, or publication date.

The basic search strategies, just described, have been successfully implemented as innovative search features in numerous online search services, such as online library catalogs, databases, and search engines. As users of services such as Amazon™, Google™, Yahoo!®, and others, you expect to find consistent interfaces, efficiency, precision, and ease of searching whether you browse online library catalogs for library publications or Amazon to purchase cameras. Some of the search strategy features are sampled below, with more details in Chapters 4 through 8 (factual resources, library catalogs, online databases, and search engines).

Google, for example, as well as other search engines have built-in sophisticated modification features that let you refine your strategy in order to get precise search results. Some of these helpful features are to limit your search to a specific language, format (e.g., pdf, ppt, ps, rtf), and time (from past 24 hours to past year). Google will also expand your result by finding similar pages as well as pages that link to the page you just found. It is best to consult online advanced tutorials for specific ways to broaden or narrow down your search (e.g., <www.google.com/help/basics.html> or <www.google.com/advanced_search?hl=en>).

Google search also offers to find you results "with all of the words," "with the exact phrase," or "with at least one of the words." Phrase searching is another specific type of search used to find sources that contain two or more adjacent words in a single character string. Using quotes around search phrases (i.e., "search innovations") will look up sites that contain the specific string included in the quotes. These are just some of the search techniques and tips that are available to you in order to get results as broad or as narrow as your need requires.

EXERCISE 3.5: Terms differ from concepts

Group the following words or phrases into two separate groups so that you can combine these two groups with the AND operator:

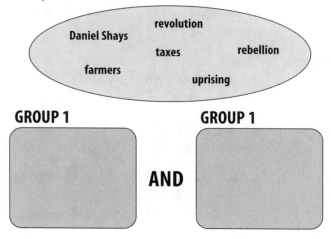

GROUP 1

GROUP 1

AND

What you have learned

Chapter 3 has introduced you to the concept of search strategy, a set of search instructions that are understood by a retrieval system, as well as to different types of search strategies; these are the known-item search, which is often used to quickly probe the scope of the literature; and the building-block search, which identifies blocks or main concepts of the search, and then combines the blocks using the operators: AND, OR, NOT. Each of these three operators tells the system how to link search words. The AND operator narrows down your search by looking for only those documents that must deal with both concepts on each side of the operator AND; the OR operator broadens the search results by having more words to choose from; the NOT operator limits your search results by excluding particular words. The chapter also discusses ways to modify a search by means of using narrower and broader search words to focus or expand the search results.

This section summarizes the most important terms and concepts that have been introduced in Chapter 3.

AND, OR, NOT operators
Each of these three operators is used to tell the system how to link search words. The AND operator narrows down your search (examples: fiction AND science; gardens AND herb; fashion AND France); the OR operator broadens the search results (examples: journals OR magazines;

Cezanne OR Pissarro); the NOT operator limits your search results (examples: gardens NOT Roman; berries NOT preserves; pottery NOT clay).

Building-block search   Search strategy that identifies BLOCKS or main concepts of the search, and then combines the blocks using the operators AND, OR, NOT.

Known-item search   Search strategy that is often used to verify and locate publications in a given collection you know by author (creator) or title.

Modifying search   Uses operators with narrower and broader search words to focus or expand the search results.

Search strategy   A set of search instructions that are understood by the retrieval system you search.

Introduction to teachers and media specialists: Search strategy is described in Chapter 3 because it applies to any of the electronic sources that might be used in research projects: online library catalogs, electronic encyclopedias, online magazine and newspaper databases, as well as the Web. Search strategy has been traditionally included with online library catalogs and online magazine databases. However, as a brainstorming tool, it applies to all types of searching ranging from printed sources to the Web.

Under the general guidelines of curricular frameworks for high school students for grades 9-12 (NAEP), history/social science students are required to demonstrate (1) chronological and spatial thinking skills; (2) historical research, evidence, and point of view; and (3) historical interpretation skills. This has direct implications for the design of information literacy programs. Among other things, it means that the students will learn to: (1) use multiple resources (e.g., textual, geographical, statistical in printed and electronic media); (2) differentiate between primary and secondary sources; (3) evaluate Web documents; (4) communicate, analyze, describe, classify, and apply information from selected sources to their projects.

> United States Department of Education. National Assessment Governing Board. (1998). *Civics framework for the 1998 National Assessment of Educational Progress, NAEP Civics.* Washington, D. C.: The Board.

An important part of searching techniques is understanding how to combine search terms into various search strategies. Next, we show examples for the two types of search strategies that are used in most online systems.

Basic Operators: AND—The example below is the use of the AND operator. It ANDs concept A (folksongs) and concept B (Germany) and creates a set of documents in the shaded area or the **intersection,** where each document must deal both with the concept folksongs and the concept Germany. The effect of the AND operator is that it reduces the size of the retrieved set; this can be helpful if you initially obtain too many items.

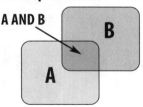

Basic Operators: OR—This type of operator, known as the OR operator, creates the union of at least two terms. An example is the union of two terms, POMPEII or HERCULANEUM. The **union** creates a set of entries each of which deals with either term A (Pompeii) or term B (Herculaneum) or both. The effect of this operator is to broaden your search, so as to give you more items.

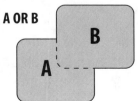

Worked out example: Search strategies described and annotated

Putting Basic Operators Together: Put all words that represent a certain concept together in a single square; link them with an OR operator. Example: a single concept might be CITIES in the Roman Empire. "OR" all individual cities:

> Rome OR Pompeii OR Herculaneum OR Naples

Repeat with other concepts, such as ARCHITECTURE. "OR" all individual words and phrases that fall under the concept of architecture and put them in a single square. Example:

> forum OR baths OR temples OR arches OR gardens

Connect these two boxes with the AND operator. If you use this strategy to search library catalogs, the result will be books that talk about architectural objects (e.g., forums, baths, temples, arches, or gardens) in ancient cities such as Pompeii, Rome, Herculaneum, or Naples. If you use the same strategy to search online magazine databases, the result will be articles and reviews in magazines and journals on the same topic from current perspectives. Finally, you can apply the same strategy to search the Web. The result will be multimedia full documents with texts, pictures, maps, tables, flags, graphs, and so on. Take note of who wrote the document, the purpose it was written for, the date of writing, and the evidence presented!

Exercise: Search strategy exercise:

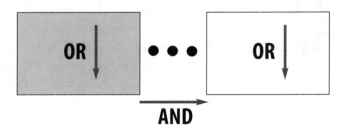

CHAPTER

4

Fact Finding: Words, Concepts, Events, Places

In this chapter, you will learn:

- Differences between dictionaries and encyclopedias: uses, features, and types
- Other fact finding sources: almanacs, directories, handbooks, and maps
- Types of information needs that are suitable for dictionaries, encyclopedias, almanacs, directories, handbooks, and maps

This chapter is divided into two sections: the first section focuses on dictionaries and encyclopedias; the second section covers other fact finding sources, also known as factbooks. These include almanacs, yearbooks, handbooks, directories, and geographical sources, such as maps, atlases, and gazetteers. These sources contain specific pieces of information and often combine compilations of factual and statistical data about places, nations, persons, and events. You are probably familiar with some of the titles: *Bartlett's Familiar Quotations*, *Facts about the Presidents*, *Kane's Famous First Facts*, *The World Almanac and Book of Facts*, *Webster's New Geographical Dictionary*, or the *World Book Encyclopedia*.

Dictionaries and encyclopedias

This section discusses different types of dictionaries and encyclopedias, how to use them, and the way they fit into the larger picture of other reference sources. You will see that many of the dictionaries and encyclopedias are becoming available on the Internet.

Different types of questions lead to different types of factbooks. Consider the following questions: where can I find . . . ?

1. An overview article about Dorothea Dix (rain forests, global warming, immigration)
2. Information about Boston (Massachusetts)
3. Rankings of liberal arts colleges in New York (or any state)
4. What is the birthplace of Apollo and Artemis

For example, to answer the first question, which type of reference source (printed or electronic) would be most suitable? Don't worry about specific titles in this exercise. (HINT: try *encyclopedias*).

Answers:

Question 2: (Boston) _____

Question 3: (liberal arts colleges)_____

Question 4: (birthplace of Apollo and Artemis)_____

Dictionaries defined

Dictionaries, also known as word books, have several meanings:

Dictionary n., *pl.* -ies. [Med. Lat. *dictionarium* < Lat. *dictio*, diction.] 1. A reference book having an explanatory alphabetical list of words, with information given for each word, including meaning, pronunciation, etymology, and often usage guidance. 2. A book listing the words of a language with translations into another language. 3. A book listing linguistic items, as words, with specialized information about them <a legal *dictionary*> <a biographical *dictionary*> 4. Computer Sci. A list stored in machine-readable form for reference by an automatic system. (*Webster's II New Riverside University Dictionary*, 1984, p. 375)

This definition makes a distinction between several types of dictionaries: general language dictionaries (e.g., monolingual English language dictionaries); bi- and polyglot dictionaries (e.g., English-Spanish dictionaries, and those that list more than two languages); as well as specialized and technical dictionaries (e.g., *The New Grove Dictionary of Music and Musicians*; *Dictionary of the Environment*). Regardless of the type of dictionary, major elements in most dictionaries include: the definition of words, spelling and alternate spelling, word origin (etymology), usage, pronunciation, syllabification, grammatical information, synonyms, antonyms, homonyms, abbreviations, slang, places, people, events, and topics.

Characteristics of dictionaries

It is useful to think about dictionaries in terms of four main characteristics. With regard to **time**, there are current usage dictionaries that list contemporary language and slang as well as historical dictionaries that trace words to the earliest known usage. With regard to **medium** of implementation, there is a growing number of dictionaries that are available as printed books and on the Internet. Level of **detail** is another main characteristic that makes dictionaries so varied. Think of a topic and chances are that you will find dictionaries on a variety of specialized topics.

We begin with some dictionary titles that you probably recognize and use. Under the heading English language dictionaries, you will notice several classes of dictionaries: "desk" or "college" dictionaries are typically one-volume English language dictionaries that will be sufficient for secondary schools. "Unabridged dictionaries" are typically large in size and scholarly in nature. We have listed two representative titles in this class of dictionaries. *The Oxford English Dictionary* (OED) is an example of a scholarly dictionary where each word is put in historical context and traced to the oldest known usage.

■ Examples of English language general dictionaries are:

- **Desk or college dictionaries**

  American Heritage College Dictionary. 4th ed. Boston: Houghton Mifflin, 2007.

  Webster's Ninth New Collegiate Dictionary. Rev. ed. Springfield, Mass.: Merriam-Webster, 2001.

- **Unabridged (fully developed) dictionaries**

  Webster's Third New International Dictionary of the English Language. Springfield, Mass.: Merriam-Webster, 2002. The Dictionary is a part of the Internet's version of the *Encyclopedia Britannica* (by subscription) at: <http://school.eb.com>.

- **Etymological dictionary**

  The Oxford English Dictionary. J. A. Simpson and E. S. C. Weiner, eds. 2d ed. Oxford: Clarendon Press, 1989, 20 vols. Supplements.

- **Slang dictionaries**

  Chapman, Robert L., ed. *American Slang*, 2nd ed. New York: Harper Perennial, 1998.

  The New Partridge Dictionary of Slang and Unconventional English. 2 v. London, Routledge, 2006.

  Check definitions of common words and jargon phrases such as "hippie," "a lame duck," "leak," "lettuce," and "hi."

- **Synonyms, Antonyms, Abbreviations**

  Roget's International Thesaurus. 6th ed. New York: HarperResource, 2001. The Internet's version of *Roget's Thesaurus* is <http://www.thesaurus.com/>.

Think of a word, say "abuse." Here is a two-step procedure for using the *Thesaurus*. Look up the word in the Index Guide in the back of the volume; notice a cluster of words (i.e., deceive 547.5; maltreat 649.7; misuse 679.2, etc.). Choose the reference you want, say, maltreat; go to entry 649.7 in the text section; under 649, it reads badness, and also refers you to see entry 648, which is its opposite, goodness. Under the decimal .7, you will find the words grouped according to their ideas rather than alphabetically like in other dictionaries. Search the word "abuse" in the Internet's version.

- Examples of some of the subject or technical dictionaries are:

    Allaby, M. ed. *Dictionary of Ecology*. 3rd. rev. Oxford: Oxford University Press, 2006.

    Dorland's Illustrated Medical Dictionary. 31st ed. Philadelphia: W.B. Saunders, 2007.

    New Grove Dictionary of Music and Musicians. 2nd ed. New York: Grove, 2001.

    The *Grove Dictionary of Music and Musicians* Online <www.grovemusic.com>, is more an encyclopedia than dictionary. The online version incorporates entries on opera and jazz, as well as musical world cultures and women composers. Special features include illustrations, audio examples, articles, and links to MP3 files.

Finally, dictionaries and encyclopedias are currently available in bundled online services as free of charge and for fee databases. For example, you may want to explore the following dictionaries on the Web:

    American Heritage Dictionary of the English Language <www.bartleby.com/61/>

    Merriam-Webster Collegiate Dictionary <www.m-w.com/>

    Oxford American Thesaurus of Current English <www.oxfordreference.com/>

    WordSmyth Dictionary - Thesaurus <www.wordsmyth.nrt/>

My students taught me what they liked the most: you just search "define <word>" in order to get a display of various definitions of the word you are looking up.

Encyclopedias defined

Encyclopedia or encyclopaedia n. [Med. Lat. *encyclopaedia*, general education course.] A comprehensive reference work having articles on a broad range of subjects or on numerous aspects of a given field, usually arranged alphabetically (*Webster's II New Riverside University Dictionary*, 1984 p. 430).

Encyclopedias are used to find: an overview article on people, historical events, ideas, topics ranging from arts, crafts, sports, and hobbies to sciences, health, and technology—a good place to begin your research exploration (see Figure 1.7 in Chapter 1). Encyclopedias also include reference sources for further reading and related material, subject headings, cross references, illustrations, maps, photographs, and charts, as well as factual data.

- Examples of types of questions suitable for encyclopedias are:
    - An overview article on Jane Addams (any significant historical, scientific, artistic, cultural figure).

- A report on tropical forests; those in the Ndoki region of central Africa are of special interest.
- An overview article on Peru (any country).
- The impact of acid rain in different countries in North America (United States, Canada, Mexico).

EXERCISE 4.1: Looking up an encyclopedia article

Take any general printed or Web-based encyclopedia, e.g., *World Book Encyclopedia*, *Encarta*, or *Encyclopedia Britannica*, printed or online <school.eb.com>.

1. Try to find an article on **Jane Addams**, a 19th century social theorist and reformer.

2. Take note of the special types of features, such as pictures, photographs, maps, as well as a list of acronyms, biographical sketches, the bibliography at the end of the article, an index, and introductory notes.

Main types of encyclopedias

The main types of encyclopedias are: general or comprehensive encyclopedias and subject or technical encyclopedias. The *World Book Encyclopedia* is a multivolume general work; entries are arranged alphabetically, so that articles on Hemingway, Honduras, and Hopi language will all be found in the volume labeled with an H. The encyclopedia is simple to use, with clear explanations of unfamiliar topics, places, and people.

- Example of a general or comprehensive encyclopedia is:

  The New Encyclopedia Britannica, 15th ed. Chicago: Encyclopedia Britannica, 2002, 32 v. (Britannica online at: <school.eb.com>).

  The *Encyclopedia Britannica* includes the following four components: index volumes; propaedia, which organizes contents into categories; micropaedia volumes consisting of short articles; and referencing to related and longer articles in the macropaedia.

- Example of subject encyclopedia is:

  The New Palgrave: A Dictionary of Economics. New York: Stockton Press, 1998. 4 v.

   As with dictionaries, many encyclopedias are now available on the Web, both free of charge and by subscription. Some examples are:

- *Columbia Encyclopedia* <www.bartleby.com/65/>

- *Jewish Encyclopedia*

- *Internet Public Library* <www.ipl.org/kidspace/browse/ref2000> includes *Britannica Concise* <concise.britannica.com> and *Encarta* online. Wikipedia <en.wikipedia.org/wiki/> has been a community-based project since 2001.

How to use encyclopedias. While dictionaries typically organize their entries alphabetically, some encyclopedias group their entries by ideas rather than alphabetically; for that reason, many encyclopedias use indexes to provide an easy access to their articles. Rule of thumb: the larger an encyclopedia, the more likely it will group entries by topics. Typically, one-volume encyclopedias arrange their entries alphabetically.

Other factual sources

This section looks at representative **factual** sources aside from dictionaries and encyclopedias. These sources contain specific pieces of information and often provide compilations of factual and statistical data about places, nations, or persons. Examples of factual sources are almanacs, yearbooks, handbooks, directories, and various geographical sources including maps, atlases, and gazetteers. You will soon learn specific titles in each of these classes of reference sources.

Factual sources, or factbooks, are used to find information about statistical data (almanacs, yearbooks); about people and organizations (handbooks, manuals, directories); and to locate geographical locations (maps, atlases, and gazetteers). Specifically, the types of questions that lead to factual sources are:

1. Addresses, phone numbers, Web home pages of scientists, famous athletes, Nobel prize winners, entertainers, congressmen, schools and colleges, new books, libraries, educational programs for high school students in the United States by school district, and so on.

2. Towns in the Brown County (Indiana) (telephone areas).

3. Health district profiles for Los Angeles County requested by a headmaster who is building a recreational facility for her high school.

Of special importance are governmental collection agencies that collect massive amounts of statistical data. These data banks are timely, well organized, updated, and free of charge. For example, **health** statistical data are available from the Department of Health and Human Services, Centers for Disease Control and Prevention (Atlanta, Georgia) at <www.cdc.gov>. If you want to track U.S. **demographics** such as home values between 1940 and 2000, the best source is U.S. Census Bureau at <www.census.gov>. **Education** related statistical sources are all compiled by the National Center for Education Statistics <nces.ed.gov> and the National Assessment of Educational Progress. More will be mentioned in Chapter 7.

Almanacs, yearbooks, handbooks, and directories defined

Almanac n. [Med. Lat. *almanach*.] 1. An annual publication including calendars with weather forecasts, astronomical information, tide tables, and other related tabular information. 2. An annual publication of lists, charts, and tables of useful information.

Yearbook n. A documentary, memorial, or historical book published every year, containing data about the previous year.

Handbooks may also contain concise information with tables, graphs, formulas, symbols; these are often written in technical language. Other handbooks may be in the areas of literature, the arts, etc.

A **directory** is a list of persons, organizations, services, or chemicals.

■ Representative examples of factbooks are:

Almanacs:

Information Please Almanac. Boston: Houghton Mifflin Co., 1974 to date. <www.infoplease.com/>. Search on specific countries such as El Salvador; what type of information does this almanac provide? Can you see a map of El Salvador? You may want to compare this almanac with the one that is written for kids: <www.factmonster.com/>.

World Almanac and Book of Facts. New York: World-Telegram, 1962- . (Annually compiled information ranging from actors to energy, U.S. history, and vital statistics).

For the Internet's version of the *Old Farmer's Almanac*, see <www.almanac.com/>.

For worldwide coverage of countries, see *CIA World FactBook* at: <www.cia.gov/cia/publications/factbook/>.

Yearbooks and handbooks:

Bartlett's Familiar Quotations. New York: Columbia University <www.bartleby.com>.

Consumer's Resource Handbook, 1992 ed. Washington DC: Office of Consumer Affairs.

Handbook of Chemistry and Physics. Boca Raton, Fla: CRC Press.

Statesman's Year-Book. New York: St. Martin's Press, 1864- .

■ Your directory guide in searching for colleges and career information:

Occupational Outlook Centers contains information for nearly 800 occupations in major areas with wages, demand, and education requirements <www.bls.gov/oco>.

Peterson's Guides to Schools is now on the Web: <www.petersons.com/>.

Princeton Review maintains its Web page with information about colleges, tests, and more: <www.review.com/>.

National Center for Education Statistics publishes surveys that are of special interest to teachers, librarians, and parents <nces.ed.gov/surveys/>. Elementary/Secondary Surveys are on Private Schools, Crime and Safety, the Census School District 2000, and many others.

For information on Internet local sources, visit the Internet Public Library Youth Division <www.ipl.org/div/kidspace> and click on USA government. Learn about the three branches, the Constitution, and state governments. Another excellent source is Los Angeles Public Library's Guide to the Web <www.lapl.org/ya>. Select "politics and government" and choose any state for local links. Federal information is divided into general information that offers access to the U.S. Government Printing Office, Statistical Abstracts of the U.S., the National Archives and Record Administration, and other resources. The Executive Branch will link you to Immigration and Naturalization Service and Social Security Administration. The Judicial Branch includes full texts from the Supreme Court Cases. There are other links to the United Nations and Embassies. Don't forget to use your telephone directories, which are full of useful sources and addresses to local offices.

Locating geographical sources

Geographical sources are maps, atlases, and gazetteers. We will begin to look at some of the representative titles in each of these sources.

A map is a representation on a flat surface of the whole earth or part of an area. While many maps are drawn on single sheets, they compile a lot of information, in fact multiple layers of information. For example, a single map might contain a base map, cultural, geophysical, and political features of a given area. In addition, it may also show names of bodies of water, streets, urban elements, and other patterns covered by the area it portrays. We list the main types of maps:

1. Area maps and atlases (by scale, maps are of large, medium, or small scale).

2. Thematic maps and atlases may be general purpose maps representing physical and cultural features, as well as special purpose maps that differ by content/theme or subject (e.g., geological, natural resources, soil, environmental, economic, demographic, health).

3. Historical maps (e.g., History of the United States) often with illustrations.

4. Gazetteers, which are dictionaries of place names.

- Examples of maps:

U. S. Geological Survey. *National Atlas of the United States*. Washington: Government Printing Office, 1970. It contains more than 300 pages of maps and a 41,000-entry index. First part has "general reference maps" (1:200 million) plus urban area maps (1:500,000), and thematic maps.

Excellent sources for maps are found bundled within online databases, such as *World Geography Index* <www.worldgeography.abc-clio.com> and *CultureGrams* <www.CultureGrams.com>. *World Geography Index* contains 217 country profiles (as of 12/20/06) ranging from Afghanistan to Zimbabwe. Each entry includes maps, flags, primary sources, biographical data and recipes, history, environment, culture, facts and figures. *CultureGrams*, published by ProQuest Information and Learning, includes 190 cultures around the world, each subdivided into 25 categories. Special features are a photo gallery, data tables, and definitions. Similarly, *SIRS Government Reporter* <sks.sirs.com> includes country profiles.

- For maps on the Internet, visit the following sites:

  <www.npac.syr.edu/textbook/kidsweb/SocialStudies/geography.html> includes an interactive Map Viewer, and U.S. Gazetteer that allow you to search for the locations of towns in the United States, and maps of the world.

  <tiger.census.gov> will give you the "Coast to Coast" digital map database; you can redraw your own maps for your neighborhood, your county, the state, etc.

  <www.lib.virginia.edu/exhibits/lewis_clark/home.html> displays maps from Columbus to Lewis and Clark's explorations.

  <www.nationalgeographic.com/mapmachine/> for topographic cartography by the National Geographic Society.

  <www.mapquest.com> allows you to find the best route from <your town> to any other town in the continental United States.

- Examples of atlases and gazetteers:

  Chambers World Gazetteer. Cambridge: Cambridge University Press, 1990.

  National Geographic Atlas of the World, 6th ed. Washington: National Geographic Society, 1992.

  Rand McNally New Cosmopolitan World Atlas, Census ed. Chicago: Rand McNally, 1991.

  Historical Atlas of the United States. Marc C. Carnes, ed.; cartography, Malcolm A. Swanson. New York: Routldge, 2003.

EXERCISE 4.2: Looking up maps

Visit a map collection in your library and locate maps of:

1. El Salvador, Nicaragua, and Mexico (any country).

2. For each country, locate major cities, bodies of water, and mountains.

3. How do you find things on a map? Does it provide a legend, an index, textual information, and any other explanations?

What you have learned

Key points to remember about factual sources include:

- The type of reference sources.

- Appreciation of a variety of factual sources that exist in different media.

- What sorts of questions are most suitable for encyclopedias, almanacs, and directories.

- How to use the Internet to locate various statistical data, tables, and compilations.

Readers are referred to consult Appendix P for an overview on how to evaluate reference books (especially relevant for resources that are mentioned in Chapters 4 and 5).

CHAPTER

Fact Finding: People, Reviews, Criticism

In this chapter, you will learn how to:

- Use different types of biographical sources in your library research
- Make use of reviews and other factual material
- Differentiate between reviews and literary criticism
- Search library catalogs for book-length biographies

A day hardly passes when you don't read about people in the news, ranging from presidents, to people in entertainment, artists, athletes, ordinary people, and deceased people. Where do we find information about people?

In this chapter, you will also learn how to use reviews. People use reviews all the time as aids in selecting what to read, hear, and see. Some people are just interested in what critics have to say about various literary and artistic productions. Before you go to a theater to listen to Tchaikovsky's opera, *The Queen of Spades*, you wish to read a bit about the composer, his work, and the society he lived in. You want to buy a book for your youngest brother. You want something that will answer those timeless questions such as how did the camel get its hump? The leopard his spots? And exactly who invented words? Where do you turn to?

In addition, literary criticism can be a valuable reference source, especially when used to substantiate an opinion or perspective on a subject. This chapter will introduce you to important biographical sources, reviews, and literary criticism.

Biographical sources

Biographical sources are used to verify the spelling of names, to find biographical data (biographical dictionaries, yearbooks, almanacs), and to locate general information about a person (biographical dictionaries).

For the moment, remember that there are many different types of biographical sources each of which is designed to answer specific questions. Don't worry about individual titles; we will cover those shortly. Choose a few people that you find intriguing (e.g., contemporary African-American poet Maya Angelou; Abigail Adams; Samuel Langhorne Clemens, known as Mark Twain; Ernest Hemingway). You need to write a one-page essay for each of the persons. What are some of the questions you need to answer? HINT: Is the person living? Is the person living in the U.S.? Consider the person's gender and profession.

Recall the road map (Figure 1.7 in Chapter 1) that illustrates the relative place of biographical sources compared to other reference books in your hypothetical search process. Typically, your search will start with encyclopedias and dictionaries. Each of these sources contains some information about people but does not go into great detail. An exception is the library catalog, which gives access to book-length biographies.

Characteristics of biographical sources

Biographical sources vary on the following five characteristics (Figure 5.1). Some include information about living people only, while others give information about both living and deceased; some biographical sources are general and cover many different professions; others might include notable women and their contributions in science alone. Some have an international slant while others consider only Americans. Biographical sources might range from giving brief data about people to full length chapters. Finally, some sources will be printed books; others may include multimedia together with interviews and excerpts from people's lives.

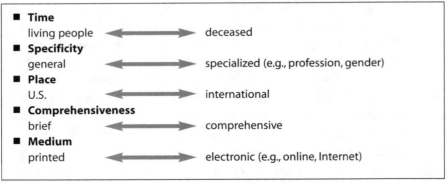

Figure 5.1: Characteristics of biographical sources

EXERCISE 5.1: Finding biographical sources

If you wish to read about Jerry Garcia (Greatful Dead), Hilary Swank (American actress), or any other personality of your choice, which of these five characteristics would you use?

Jerry Garcia:

Hilary Swank:

EXERCISE 5.2: Which source is the first best source?

Answer the following questions about the four people below by using **library catalogs, encyclopedias** (printed or on the Web), and digital primary sources from **archival** collections. For example, archival resources are rich with portraits, cartoons, early moving pictures, and textual materials such as diaries and manuscripts. For example, is Joan Didion living in the United States? What did/does she do? Which source (encyclopedia title, library book) did you use to answer these questions?

PERSON'S NAME	TIME: living: Yes / No Not sure	PLACE: U.S.: Yes / No Not sure	PROFESSION: Writer, composer, politician, teacher, activist, other	SOURCE: title of the source (year): page #
Thomas Jefferson				
Dylan Thomas				
Joan Didion				
Toni Morrisson				
George Sand*				

*Find Belinda Jack's biography of George Sand, a 19th century French novelist, befriended by Chopin, Liszt, Delacroix, Balzac, and Flaubert. Reviews appeared in the *New York Times Book Review*, and other papers. Read about her artistic developments and intellectual atmosphere in early 19th century France.

Organization of biographical sources

Biographical sources may be divided into two large groups: sources about **living people** and those about **deceased people**. Each of these two sources may be subdivided into U.S. general and specialized sources and world general and specialized sources. Below, we give examples for these types of biographical sources. In addition, there are some general Internet links that you might want to explore:

- <lii.org/> then click on **People**: **Arts and Humanities**; **Literature**, then on **Authors** by region.
  When was Maya Angelou born?

  _____

-
  What is Al Gore's full name?
  Your answer:

  _____

  When was Pinochet the president of Chile? Is he alive?
  Your answer:

  _____

- <www.ipl.org> compiles numerous links to biographical sources under **Artists and Architects**; **Authors**; **Entertainers**; **Musicians and Composers**; **Politicians and Rulers**; **Scientists and Inventors**. This site includes biographical references in the following categories: African-American History; American Women's History: A Research Guide; Distinguished Women of Past and Present; Spanish-language resources for biographies of famous people from all over the world including royalty and world leaders, writers, actors, musicians and singers, artists, athletes, Nobel Prize winners, and more.

Living people

An example of a general printed biographical source for persons living in the U.S. is *Who's Who in America*. In addition, there are a variety of specialized *Who's Who* biographical sources (e.g., in American Politics; Aviation and Aerospace; Golf; Science and Technology). An example of a specialized biographical source is:

- *American Men & Women of Science: A biographical dictionary of today's leaders in physical, biological, and related sciences*, 23rd ed. Farmington Hills, Mich.: Thomson Gale, 2007.

- *Contemporary Authors: A bio-bibliographical guide to current writers in fiction, general nonfiction, poetry, journalism, drama, motion pictures, television, and other fields* (Thomson Gale) provides both living and deceased commissioned autobiographies by leading writers; it also contains analytical bibliographical essays. Check the following Web site for biographical information:

The Cambridge Biographical Encyclopedia with about 15,000 entries; it is on the Web at:

EXERCISE 5.3: Looking up brief biographical information

■ Find anything about Barack Obama (his age, birth place, which schools did Obama graduate from, professional titles, etc.).

Question for bonus points:

■ Does your library have any books authored by Barack Obama?

Yes ☐   No ☐

Deceased people

In addition to obituaries in newspapers and journals, both printed and electronic, the following sources are useful to locate information about deceased persons:

■ U.S. general and specialized sources:

Dictionary of American Biography. New York: Scribner, 1928-37.

Notable American Women, 1607-1950. A Biographical Dictionary. Cambridge, Mass.: Belknap Press of Harvard University Press, 1971-2004, 5 v.

■ World general and specialized sources:

Dictionary of Scientific Biography. New York: Scribner, 1970-1990, supplements.

Encyclopedia of Women Social Reformers/Helen Rappaport. Santa Barbara, Calif.: ABC-CLIO, 2001.

Merriam Webster's Biographical Dictionary. Springfield, Mass.: Merriam-Webster, 1995.

Before using any source, biographical included, it is useful to scan through preface and index sections. The former tells us selection choices for including certain persons from the source. As an example, the preface of the *Encyclopedia of Women Social Reformers* tells us that "some ruthless decisions" were made on whom to include in the *Encyclopedia* based on nationality, issues in which women were involved, and time period (roughly from the French Revolution, 1789 to the 1970s). By skimming the index, readers can quickly find out which women are included. Reading preface notes and indices for online sources is equally important. The term preface is often called "description" or "about" a given source or an online database.

Nowadays, many publishers offer printed and online versions of the same work, including both living and deceased people in a given profession; many are international in scope, comprehensive in time coverage and completeness. Among the widely used biographical sources is Gale Cengage's InfoTrac® databank <http://infotrac.galegroup.com/>. This resource, by subscription only, can be searched by knowing the author's name, title of a given work, or by typing in keywords; for example, the following entry will be retrieved as a result of simply typing in **virginia woolf** in a search box:

Virginia Woolf (1882-1941)

Variant(s): Adeline Virginia Stephen; Adeline Virginia Woolf; Virginia Stephen; Virginia Adeline Woolf; Virginia Stephen Woolf; Adeline Virginia Stephen Woolf

Nationality: British; English

Genre(s): Bildungsroman; Biographical sketches; Diaries; Essays; Experimental fiction; Letters (Correspondence); Literary criticism; Novels; Short stories

Literary Movement/Time Period: Bloomsbury Group, English modern period (Literature), Feminist criticism, Practical criticism

Woolf, (Adeline) Virginia **"(Adeline) Virginia Woolf," in *Contemporary Authors*. (A profile of the author's life and works)**
Woolf, Virginia **"Virginia Woolf," in *Dictionary of Literary Biography, Volume 36: British Novelists, 1890-1929: Modernists*. A Bruccoli Clark Layman Book. Edited by Thomas F. Staley, University of Tulsa. The Gale Group, 1985, pp. 292-313.**
Woolf, Virginia **"Virginia Woolf," in *Dictionary of Literary Biography, Volume 162: British Short-Fiction Writers, 1915-1945*. A Bruccoli Clark Layman Book. Edited by John H. Rogers, Vincennes University. The Gale Group, 1996, pp. 357-371.**
Woolf, Virginia **"Virginia Woolf," in *Dictionary of Literary Biography, Volume 100: Modern British Essayists, Second Series*. A Bruccoli Clark Layman Book. Edited by Robert Beum, The Gale Group, 1990, pp. 336-346.**

As we noted earlier, there are certain decision making questions that are useful to think about regardless of the medium we are searching, whether Web-based resources like Thomson Gale databases, printed books, or online library catalogs. Some of these "prompts" relate to the following:

- Date or era

- Ethnicity (e.g., African-American, Asian American, Hispanic American)

- Literary genre (e.g., Adventure Fiction, American Romanticism, Antislavery Literature, Avant-Garde, Vampire Fiction, Women)

- Literary movement (e.g., Age of Goethe, Harlem Renaissance, Jazz Poetry)

Another example is Oxford University Press that publishes *Grove Dictionary of Music and Musicians* (both a multivolume reference work as well as an online subscription database <www.grovemusic.com>). *The Grove online* contains more than 45,000 articles on people, instruments, and styles from baroque to blues and jazz. Articles are written by more than 6,000 international contributors. Some of the features include 5,000 links to images and more than 500 audio musical examples. In addition, world musical cultures are a nice addition to the work; African, Asian, South American, and Jewish musical styles are well represented.

General remarks. If you are hunting for book-length biographies, search your library catalogs. Specifically, to get book-length biographies from your school library catalog, simply type in a person's name; if you are searching larger library catalogs, you may want to attach the following subheadings to persons' names.

Examples:

NAME of the person you are researching, and add any of the following:

biography	in literature
correspondence	manuscripts
criticism and interpretation	technique
fiction	youth
interviews	style
quotations	

To get biographical information from magazine articles, search ProQuest. You will find current information from newspaper articles <www.latimes.com/, http://nytimes.com/>. For information on less-known people around the world, check search engines, such as <www.google.com>.

Why would you look for a (book) review?

Reviews are used for a variety of reasons. Consider the following examples:

1. To see what critics say about a book (to get critical evaluations or opinions on a work, style, character, and sometimes biographical data).

2. To understand what a book is about (to get a summary of the work, plot, key issues raised). Here, summaries are usually descriptive rather than evaluative.

3. To aid in selecting which works to read or which performances to see.

4. To get a quick reference for a work's characters, dates of premiers, and cast.

5. To obtain biographical information about the author.

The purpose of a review is to give people an accurate idea of a work, such as film, book, play, dance performance, or exhibit, so that they may be more knowledgeable prior to seeing the film or purchasing the book. A review is different from a critique. Reviews announce films, books, and plays; describe topics and methods; discuss technical qualities, actors, directors; and examine its merits compared to other similar works. Reviews usually appear shortly after the publication or the production. Many books are never reviewed. In contrast, a critique is far more evaluative than a review; the critique usually writes about works that already have some standing and assumes that the reader has already seen the work.

Some of the most important sources for book reviews are newspapers, such as *Los Angeles Times*, *New York Times*, *Washington Post*; magazines including *Time*, *Newsweek*, *Cosmopolitan*, academic journals, as well as review publications (*Science Books & Films*, *Choice*, *New York Review of Books*, *New York Times Book Review*). Many of these sources are on the Web <lii.org/>. Then choose <u>Literature</u> and <u>Reviews</u>.

The most widely used review sites are:

BookWire <www.bowker.com/bookwire/reviews.asp>
Booklist <www.ala.org/booklist/index.html>
New York Times Book Review <www.nytimes.com/books/>
New York Review of Books <www.nybooks.com>

NOTE: Remember to cite sources for review articles in your reports.

EXERCISE 5.4: Source(s) for current book reviews

Q1: Where would you look for a current book (theater, movie, concert) review?

A1: _____

Q2: What is the difference between a book review and a critique? Please write your answers in the space below:

Literary criticism

The purpose of literary criticism is to evaluate literary works by novelists, screenwriters, poets, short story writers, playwrights, and science fiction and nonfiction writers. Furthermore, it may involve studying the authors' lives, comparing and contrasting different writing styles, ideas, motifs, and symbolism used in a work, or applying theory to texts or movements in literature.

Some of the sources that may help start your search for information are encyclopedias and library catalogs. A more specialized source is the *Columbia Dictionary of Modern Literary and Cultural Criticism*. Another prominent reference book that defines and discusses terms, critical theories, and points of view that are commonly applied to the classification, analysis, interpretation, and history of works of literature is *A Glossary of Literary Terms*.

If you search library catalogs for books on literary criticism, you will find the following subject headings (LCSH) useful in your exploration:

American Literature--United States
American Literature--United States--20th Century
American Literature--United States--Women Authors
American Prose Literature--Colonial period, ca 1600-1775
American Prose Literature--History and Criticism
Children's Literature
Criticism--History
Criticism--History--20th Century
Literary Criticism in the Renaissance

Figure 5.2: Search for books on literary criticism

In addition to some of the sources that were noted earlier in this chapter, here we list just a few more sources for literary criticism:

- *Contemporary Literary Criticism. Excerpts from criticism of the works of today's novelists, poets, playwrights, short story writers, scriptwriters, and other creative writers.* Detroit: Gale Research, 1973- .

- Magill, Frank N. *Masterplots*, rev. ed. Englewood Cliffs, NJ: Salem Press, 1976, 12 vols. *Survey of Contemporary Literature*, rev. ed., 1976, 12 v.

Gale Cengage's Literature Resource Center (LRC) online includes (per publisher's factsheet):

- Biographical entries on more than 130,000 authors, from *Contemporary Authors, Contemporary Authors New Revisions, Dictionary of Literary Biography, Contemporary Literary Criticism,* and other Gale sources, providing detailed biographical, bibliographical, and contextual information about authors' lives and works

- More than 70,000 selected full-text critical essays and reviews from *Contemporary Literary Criticism, Classical and Medieval Literature Criticism, Literature Criticism from 1400-1800, Nineteenth-Century Literature Criticism, Twentieth-Century Literary Criticism*, as well as *Drama Criticism, Poetry Criticism, Shakespearean Criticism, Short Story Criticism* and *Children's Literature Review*

- More than 7,000 overviews of frequently studied works, from sources including Gale's For Students series, *Literature and Its Times* and *Characters in 20th-Century Fiction*

- More than 650,000 full-text articles, critical essays and reviews from more than 300 scholarly journals and literary magazines

- Nearly 30,000 full-text poems, short stories, and plays

- More than 4,500 interviews

- Nearly 5,000 links to selected Web sites and more than 2,800 author portraits

- The ability to identify groups of authors who share characteristics such as genre, time period, themes, nationality, ethnicity, and gender

- *Merriam-Webster's®️ Encyclopedia of Literature*, featuring 10,000 definitions of literary terms

According to the Gale Cengage's factsheet, material from forthcoming volumes of Gale's print literature series are added to Literature Resource Center throughout the year, along with full-text journal articles and Web sites. Web sites are checked and death dates, major awards, major literary works, newsworthy events, and career-related events are added to biographical essays to keep content accurate and reliable.

Literature Resource Center subscribers can choose to add any of the following products as fully integrated modules:

- Scribner Writers series, a collection of more than 2,200 original, detailed bio-critical essays on the lives and works of important authors from around the world

- Twayne's Authors series, featuring the content of nearly 600 books in three print series, this series offers in depth introductions to the lives and works of writers, the history and influence of literary movements and the development of literary genres

- *The Modern Language Association (MLA) International Bibliography*, the world's foremost subject index for books and articles published on modern languages, literatures, folklore, and linguistics since 1926. Literature Resource Center subscribers who add the MLA International Bibliography also get the MLA International Bibliography on InfoTrac as a standalone database at no extra cost

The Contemporary Literary Criticism (CLC) series of printed volumes includes critical commentaries on more than 2,000 authors now living or who died after December 31, 1959. Each CLC volume contains about 500 individual excerpts taken from numerous book review periodicals, general magazines, scholarly journals, and books. Entries provide critical evaluations spanning from the beginning of an author's career to the most current commentary. Entries also include portraits when available, principal works, explanatory notes, and, whenever possible, previously unpublished interviews. Further readings appear at the end of entries on authors for whom a significant amount of criticism exists in addition to the pieces reprinted in CLC.

SIRS Knowledge Source database <sks.sirs.com>, via ProQuest, offers a wide range of biographical sources for you to explore. Besides this database, which will be described shortly, there are many other online sources for biographical information; examples are EBSCOhost <web.ebscohost.com> and JSTOR <www.jstor.org>.

The SIRS database, mentioned above, consists of three components:

- SIRS® Researcher

- SIRS® Government Reporter

- SIRS® Renaissance

While the *Researcher* component focuses on issues, current events, maps of the world, and ideas for research topics (e.g., cloning, stem-cell research, same-sex marriage, history of Islam), the *Government Reporter* offers information on country profiles, federal agencies, U.S. Congress, U.S. presidents, U.S. Supreme Court, historical documents, and the National Archives documents. Of particular interest to this chapter is the *Renaissance* component. Among the links is "Literary Corner," which leads us to 277 prominent worldwide authors, covering numerous literary genres, regions, and periods. A search for any given writer results in 20 to 30 entries from magazines and newspapers, reference books and graphical material. The tab on "Literary Profiles" from the same screen has headings on American and English Literature, Contemporary Literature, Literary Criticism, and online e-books. From there, we can connect to biographical and literary criticism writings about 277 authors with full–texts of their works.

For example, in order to read Jane Austin's *Emma*, we are automatically given the link to the appropriate entry in the California Digital Library <sunsite.berkeley.edu/Literature/Austen/Emma/>. For those wishing to read a free hypertext e-book edition of Oscar Wilde's novel *The Picture of Dorian Gray*, visit <www.upword.com/wilde/dorgray.html>. Numerous other literary full–texts are given at the Humanities Text Initiative at the University of Michigan digital library <www.hti.umich.edu/index-all.html>.

Specific writers and their literary work are well represented on the Internet. For example, for an overview of Shakespeare's plays, resources, and online editions of his works, check the Web's first edition of the *Complete Works of Shakespeare* at <www-tech.mit.edu/Shakespeare/works.html>.

What you have learned

1. Key points to remember about the various biographical, review, and literary criticism sources include: what biographical sources are, and how they are represented in library catalogs, online databases, and archives.

2. Understanding the major differences that exist between reviews and literary criticism.

3. What type of questions are most suitable for biographical sources, for reviews, and for literary criticism material.

4. How to use library catalogs to find out which length-size biographical sources are available.

5. How to use online services, such as Gale Cengage's InfoTrac, ProQuest, as well as the Web, to locate various reviews and biographical sources.

CHAPTER

Finding Works in Library Collections

In this chapter, you will learn how:

- To search library catalogs for books, maps, and other reference sources
- To interpret data in library catalog entries
- To apply different search strategies for different information needs

This chapter will introduce you to the effective uses of library catalogs in general. You will search for books, DVDs, CDs, atlases, and reference materials in your local library catalog. In addition, you will learn about remote and larger library catalogs on the Internet.

What are library catalogs?

Library catalogs are sources that provide bibliographic entries to documents, such as books (NOT parts of books), CDs, DVDs, atlases, maps, and primary sources, or finding aids to primary sources. For example, Figure 6.1 (see next page) gives enough information to help you decide if the book, *Women and Gender in Early Modern Europe*, would be potentially relevant to you. By "enough information" we mean information contained in the data elements, including authors' names, publication data, physical description of the book, and subject headings. So instead of going to the library stacks and browsing books there, you first search the catalog, which will save you time and more efficiently show you the books that you need. In effect, the library catalog is for library collections what an index and table of contents are for books. They are finding, browsing, and collocating aids. To collocate means to group similar materials together.

Knowing that catalogs give access to book-like materials and not to, for example, magazine articles is critical; it is also useful to know what kind of information needs are well-suited for using library catalogs. The following are representative types of questions that may be addressed by searching library catalogs:

- Are there any illustrated collections of myths from around the world?

- Did Benjamin Franklin write any autobiographical books?

- How do you borrow from your local library a film "Le Rossignol," (DVD preferred), after Hans C. Andersen's fairy tale "The Emperor and the Nightingale" with Stravinsky's well-known music "Firebird?"

- Are there any books on women and gender in modern Europe?

- Does the library have encyclopedias on Latin-American history and culture?

Author	Wiesner, Merry E.
Title	Women and gender in early modern Europe / Merry E. Wiesner.
Published	New York : Cambridge University Press, 1993.
Description	xii, 264 p. : ill. ; 24 cm.
Series	New approaches to European history.
Subject(s)	Women--European--History.
	Women--Social conditions--History.

Figure 6.1: Cataloging entry of a book

EXERCISE 6.1: Looking up by topic

Search the library catalog and give answers to the following questions:

1. How many books did you find on **solar energy**?

2. Circle different class numbers that are given to books on solar energy:

   [5xx]   [6xx]   [3xx]   [other] write down class number

   > REMINDER: go to Chapter 3 to see Dewey Decimal Classification (DDC) for detailed
   > subdivisions. Alternatively, see Appendices H1 and H2, or visit www.tnrdlib.bc.ca/dewey.html

3. Look at the subject headings that are assigned to the books on solar energy; are there any new
   subject headings that you may use to find more books on solar energy or a similar topic? Write
   down subject heading(s) other than solar energy that are given to books on solar energy:

   subject heading 1:

   subject heading 2:

   subject heading 3:

- OPTIONAL: Cite the book using the format for books in Chapter 9.

EXERCISE 6.2: Looking up people

Find books on **Samuel Adams**—you need information for a research report on how Samuel Adams influenced the development and growth of early American politics, government, and society. You will probably receive from your history teacher a list of other important figures from early American history.

Search for books about **Samuel Adams**.

1. How many items (books) did you find?

2. Which class numbers are they given?

> REMINDER: see Chapter 3, or click at: <www.tnrdlib.bc.ca/dewey.html> to get a description of the 10 Dewey Decimal classes.

3. Now look at several entries on your screen; what subject heading(s) are assigned to these books?

    Subject heading 1:

    Subject heading 2:

    Subject heading 3:

4. Use these subject headings to find more books on Samuel Adams or similar topics.

- Go to the library shelves and locate a book on your topic. If the book is not there, look around the missing book and locate a book on the same or similar topic.

- OPTIONAL: Cite the book in the space provided below using the format for books in Chapter 9.

EXERCISE 6.3: Looking up places

Search your local catalog for books on **Mexico:**

1. How many books did you find that are related to Mexico?

> Notice that books will cover various aspects: Mexican culture, revolutions, the art of ancient Mexico, Pre-Columbian civilizations (e.g., Aztecs and Mayas), cookery, travel, maps, literature, geography of Baja California (Mexico), customs, immigration.

2. How many books did you find in class 3xx (social sciences)?

3. Note the subject headings of the books grouped in the 3xx class; write down several subject headings:

    Subject heading 1: _____

    Subject heading 2: _____

4. How many books are in the 6xx class (technology, applied sciences)? _____

5. Search the library catalog under the heading: Art, Mexican. Are there any illustrated books in English? If so, list two titles and the corresponding call numbers below:

    Title 1:_____

    Call number: _____

    Title 2:_____

    Call number: _____

EXERCISE 6.4: Learning to read a cataloging entry

Find books on mythology; specifically, locate a book by Virginia Hamilton and answer the following questions:

1. Write down its full title including the subtitle:

   Title:

   Subtitle (part of title that follows the ":" symbol):

2. Is this book illustrated?   Yes ☐   No ☐

3. What is the call number of this book?

EXERCISE 6.5: Use library catalogs to find books; use databases to find magazine articles

1. Can you find journal articles in library catalogs? For example, can you find in your library catalog an article titled "Coral eden," by David Doubilet that appeared in *National Geographic* magazine, volume 195, number 1, January 1999?

   Yes ☐   No ☐

2. Can you locate the book described in Figure 6.1, in your library catalog?

   Yes ☐   No ☐

Main objectives of library catalogs

Library catalogs are designed:

1. To show what the library has when you know the author's (creator's) name, the title, or both. Examples: Twain's *Finn*. Fowler's *Samuel Adams: Radical Puritan*. Andersen's *The Emperor and the Nightingale*.

2. To show what the library has on a given topic. Examples: United States Declaration of Independence; solar energy; mythology.

3. To show all books by (and about) an author. Examples: Mark Twain; Maya Angelou.

4. To show what the library has in a particular form of literature, such as encyclopedias, science fiction, gothic romance, satire, cartoons. Examples: encyclopedias of Latin America.

In the first case, you will typically **know** some of the following information: the author, some title words, and perhaps a precise title. The earlier example, *Samuel Adams: Radical Puritan*, is an example of a "known-item search" where the author/title is known.

In the second case, you might know the topic or **subject**—what the book is about, hence "subject search" (United States History Revolution, 1775-1783). To search library catalogs by subject, libraries use **subject authority files**. An example of such a file is the Library of Congress Subject Headings (LCSH), discussed in Chapter 2. The purpose is to bring together all variants under one subject heading so that the material about the same or similar subjects can be brought together in one place. Consequently, documents that are represented with synonymous terms to mean the same thing—lawyers, attorneys, counsel—can be looked for under one subject heading in the catalog rather than scattered alphabetically under the three headings (i.e., lawyers, attorneys, counsel).

The third feature is unique to library catalogs. Maya Angelou's works might be found under M. Angelou, Maya Angelou, or some other variation. Library catalogs establish and maintain one name for each author, so that you can find everything that he or she has published under that one name. The example Figure 6.2 shows a typical case of a well-known American writer, Samuel Langhorne Clemens, who wrote under his more popular name, Mark Twain. So, even if you did not know Twain's real name, you would retrieve all his publications from the library catalog.

> Clemens, Samuel Langhorne, 1835-1910
> SEARCH: Twain, Mark, 1835-1910

Figure 6.2: Name Authority File

The fourth feature of library catalogs assists in locating the precise type of literature on a desired topic. Examples include dictionaries and encyclopedias, interpretation and criticism, and fiction.

EXERCISE 6.6: Search library catalogs under different access points

1. Try to locate the publication below in your library:

Author:	Walser, Robert.
Title:	Running with the devil : power, gender, and madness in heavy metal music / by Robert Walser.
Published:	Hanover, NH : University Press of New England, 1993.
Description:	xviii, 222 p. ; ill. ; 24 cm.
Series:	Music/culture
Subject:	Heavy metal (Music)--History and criticism.

2. How would you search the above book in your library catalog by author?
   Answer:

3. How would you search the above book in your library catalog by title?
   Answer:

4. How would you search for books on the same/similar topic in your library catalog?
   Answer:

5. Using the Dewey Decimal Classification (see Chapter 2), where would you find this book in the library? Mark only one box of the four possibilities below:

   ☐ class 500 (science/metals)   ☐ class 700 (arts/music)

   ☐ class 600 (applied science)   ☐ class 300 (social studies/culture)

Beyond your local library catalog

In order to search beyond your local library for the topics in Exercises 6.1 to 6.6, visit the following resources:

> To search for books, DVDs, CDs, and other materials worldwide, enter: <www.bookwire.com/index/libraries.html> or OCLC's WORLDCAT at <www.worldcat.org>.

Many current Web library catalogs are portals to special and archival collections. Primary source collections are especially important now when curricular standards call for critical thinking skills and the use of primary source materials in research projects. For example, to explore Online Archive of California, visit their digital collections at <www.oac.cdlib.org>. Now that you are in the Online Archives

From the Eastman's Originals Collection, Department of Special Collections, General Library, University of California, Davis. The collection is property of the Regents of the University of California; no part may be reproduced or used without permission of the Department of Special Collections.

of California, search for more than 120,000 online images that are thematically arranged under the following broad headings: history, nature, people, places, society, and technology <www.oac.cdlib.org/search.image.html>.

Selecting the NATURE heading, students can view online images of, for example, deserts. The image on page 79 is from the Online Archive of California: "Joshua Trees on Mohave Desert," dated 1945. The contributing institution is the General Library Department of Special Collections from the University of California, Davis, by the Regents of The University of California.

Images in each of the categories are described and annotated. For example, if you selected the category plants, you could find about 20 online images of various plants including fruits. Diving into fruits, we find an image below depicting a family of Japanese ancestry working in their strawberry farm just before transfer to a War Relocation Camp. This photograph, taken by Dorothea Lange (April 24, 1942), comes from the Bancroft Library, University of California, Berkeley.

This example demonstrates that today's library catalogs go beyond accessing "just books," as many students have told us. They are truly portals to recorded knowledge including published books, videorecordings, electronic books, CDs, digitized collections of photographs, interviews, folksongs, and other cultural artifacts. Because they offer access to both primary and secondary sources, they can be used for research and instructional purposes, and for different grade levels and disciplines.

Researchers have made great strides in digitizing scholarly collections including primary sources of materials so that we can use them globally in our own local libraries, including your schools and colleges. These images and other sources are well documented, described, and contextualized.

Many library catalogs are nowadays part of digital portals that invite users to search local collections in addition to remote ones. An example is the Library of Congress online catalog <catalog.loc.gov> with the options to search via a basic and an advanced search. It also gives access to digital prints and photographs <www.loc.gov/rr/print/> as well as to a sound online inventory and catalog. Gateway to an alphabetical list of online library catalogs on the Web contains catalogs for worldwide library catalogs to university, public, state, and federal library collections <www.loc.gov/z3950/gateway.html#1c>.

Putting library objectives into practice: Examples from Melvyl and beyond

This section is of particular importance to juniors and seniors as they prepare for college-level education. Educators may also be interested in searching large union online catalogs of numerous academic and research libraries. One such example for the state of California is Melvyl, a feature of the California Digital Library <melvyl.cdlib.org/>. It provides access to all major library collections of the state of California. It holds more than 27 million records from the OCLC Online Union Catalog for books, computer files, audiovisual materials, periodicals, maps, manu-scripts, and musical scores in a variety of languages. The database does not include individual articles from journals, newspapers, or book chapters.

Another library catalog, OCLC's WORLDCAT <www.worldcat.org>, gives records of books, audiovisuals, and other publications; it shows where certain items are held so that your librarians can borrow, through interlibrary loan, from other libraries.

What you have learned

Chapter 6 focuses on searching online library catalogs in general. The following themes are discussed:

1. What library catalogs are and what they contain.

2. What sort of information you would need to have in order to use catalogs effectively.

3. What information is included in a library catalog entry.

This chapter has introduced the following concepts. We review only the most important terminology:

Collocation	Grouping together documents by a well-recognizable attribute, such as grouping books by their topic, value, author, and size.
Corporate Author	A party responsible for intellectual or artistic content of works; examples are governmental agencies, associations, schools, and churches.
Melvyl	An online library catalog, produced by the University of California Office of the President; it provides access to UC library holdings, California State libraries, and many other academic and special collections in the state of California.
Name Authority File	A list of established forms of names (personal, corporate, series) that are used in searching library items.

Online Catalog

A library catalog that is searchable online. Some catalogs contain records of materials owned by several libraries. These library catalogs are known as union catalogs, such as the OCLC's WorldCat <www.worldcat.org> and MELVYL <melvyl.cdlib.org>. Union catalogs may include library records by a particular region, state, the entire nation, or by some other characteristics (e.g., all branch public libraries in a given city; library holdings of all independent school libraries in a given state, etc.).

Series

A group of separate items related to one another by the fact that each item bears, in addition to its own title proper, a collective title applying to the group as a whole. In the earlier example, "Running with the devil," there are many books that belong to the same general series titled music/culture.

CHAPTER

7

Searching & Evaluating Internet Sources

In this chapter, you will learn how:

- To search Web sources that you use in your work

- To locate basic sources that are related to your classes as well as health, education, and lifelong information needs such as finding a college and employment

The Internet has been defined as the international network of interconnected networks for data transmission and exchange. Here, we view the Internet as a worldwide digital collection of resources for exploration and research. For example, it provides access to college directories <www.petersons.com>, <www.collegegrad.com>, <www.review.com>; collections of images, maps, books, (e.g., <images.google.com>, <maps/google.com>, <books.google.com>, <scholar.google.com>); online shopping <www.amazon.com>; and the latest information on sports <espn.go.com>. The Internet has become a unique global community forum for debate, exploration, learning, entertainment, and self-development. But can it bring global peace, cut pollution, eradicate cancer and other diseases through the human genome project, and reduce inequality? For answers to some of these questions, read an article, "What the Internet cannot do," in *Economist* <www.beachbrowser.com/Archives/News-and-Human-Interest/August-2000/What-the-Internet-cannot-do.htm/>. Surely, not everything is available on the Web, which is why one of our chapters in this book focuses on the Internet and ways to search and evaluate its contents. An estimated 500 times larger than the surface of the Web is online content that search engines don't index, and therefore are hidden from the searcher. These resources are referred to as the invisible Web, also known as deep Web.

This view of the Internet makes an important distinction between the Internet as an **information resource** and the Internet as a **communication service** (e.g., e-mail, chats, blogs, wikis, podcasts, Really Simple Syndication or RSS feeds, Web portals, and other social software tools); check out Podomatic <www.podomatic.com>, Odeon <www.odeon.com>, and podcasting tools <www.podcastingnews.com/topics/Podcasting_Software.html>.

This chapter focuses on conceptual aspects of the Internet as a collection of information resources. Accordingly, Chapter 7 will focus on search engines and respective search strategies. We will use examples that will be relevant in your classes and outside of classroom activities. Exercises will give you hands-on experience in searching and evaluating networked resources. In particular, **Think Guide #4**, at the end of this chapter, summarizes criteria for evaluation of Web sources. Appendix P is an additional place to read on how to evaluate sources.

Introduction to the Internet: A brief look

The Internet is both a vast collection of information and a communication system of computer networks worldwide. All these different networks communicate with each other using the same telecommunication protocol, Transmission Control Protocol/Internet Protocol (TCP/IP). Locally, you are connected to a host computer that directly provides services regardless of the operating system of your computer or workstation. The host computer is linked through regional networks to the national backbone of networks.

Internet tools, such as the World Wide Web or the Web, now in its Web 2.0 version, allow you to access and find interlinked Hypertext-based multimedia contents. For our readers who wish to keep abreast with the latest transformations of the Web, visit Web Summit Annual Conferences <www.web2summit.com> and the related Expo <www.web2expo.com>.

There are various browsers that help you navigate and search the Internet's vast resources. Examples of the Internet's browsers include Mozilla at <www.mozilla.com> and Internet Explorer at <www.microsoft.com>. To search the Web, use various search engines, robots, and meta-search engines, including the following:

- Yahoo! at <www.yahoo.com> as well as Ask at <www.ask.com>
- Google at <www.google.com>
- Meta-search engines such as Dogpile at <www.dogpile.com>

For a detailed comparison of different search engines, see Table 7.3 in this chapter, page 97.

There are two main modes of searching the Internet's resources. For an **explorato-ry** search, use Hypertext links that will take you to related Web documents. For a more **direct** search, you need to know the address of the Web document or the Uniform Resource Locator (URL); enter it directly into the URL location area and search using specific keywords. As an example for the exploratory search, link to a subject guide directory Yahoo! <www.yahoo.com> and choose any of the broad subject classes from the main menu. These are subdivided into more specific subject categories, which in turn contain lists of Web documents on various topics, events, and other resources.

Every Web document is assigned a standardized unique address called a URL, as noted above. The address specifies the method of access (http:// for Hypertext Transmission Protocol), the address of the host (www), the computer on which the data or service is located (sjsu), and the type of domain (**edu** for education; **gov** for government; **com** for company; **org** for organization), sometimes a path/or names of files (.depts/Beethoven/). So, the entire URL for the sources about Ludwig van Beethoven is: <www.sjsu.edu/depts/Beethoven>. Web documents are typically writ-ten in HTML (Hypertext Markup Language) language and are designated with the suffix ".html." There are numerous Web tutorials and authoring sources. Here is one of many such sources: <www.cwru.edu/help/introHTML/toc.html>.

EXERCISE 7.1: Finding Web documents by browsing

Browse and discover: If you are still in Yahoo! <dir.yahoo.com>, click on one of the main categories; what subdivisions do you see on your screen? Explore other subdivisions, such as **Fitness** and **Sports** and subsequent headings on "activity calorie calculators," and "hula hooping."

1. How easy is it to find a partial list of genetically engineered foods? Does "Ultra Slim Fast®" have genetically engineered ingredients?

2. Write down the entire series of categories from the broadest to the most specific one. Describe your search in the space below:

3. Go back to the main menu. You are looking for history stuff. Which of the main categories will most likely give you information about U.S.–Mexican War (1846-1848)? Use the space below for your search description. Write down the entire sequence of choices that you made before you got your sites on the U.S.–Mexican War.

How to think critically about Web contents

Because not all Web documents are equally well suited and valuable, this section introduces you to important types of criteria that you could use to evaluate the material produced on the Web. These criteria are organized under the following four headings:

- Authority
- Content
- Structure, visual design, and interface
- Search features

Under each of these four headings, we suggest questions that will help you to evaluate Web contents.

Authority

1. Is the creator/author of the Web page given? Is there a distinction made between the author of the content, the Webmaster, the contact person, and sponsors of the site? For your information, the author is typically a person or an organization responsible for the intellectual and artistic content of the Web page; the Webmaster is typically a programmer who is responsible for coding the content into the HTML language.

2. If the author, editor, or creator of the intellectual content of the Web page is given, are links included to his or her credentials and affiliations? This is important because it gives you an opportunity to get in touch with the author in order to obtain more detailed information, explanation, and further clarification on various issues. Furthermore, knowing the authors' names, you as a searcher can explore their own Web sites for additional sources, teaching material, tests, research interests, and their published work that may not be available through search engines.

3. Which sector is represented in the domain part of the address (edu—for education, gov—for government, com—for company, org—for organization, mil—for military)? Typically, university and governmental sites are free of charge, tend to be of higher quality, and are less biased than the commercial sites. Some excellent -org Web sites are produced by non-profit organizations such as the Public Broadcasting Service, PBS <www.pbs.org>, the Internet Public Library <www.ipl.org>, and others put out and maintained by professional organizations such as the American Mathematical Society <www.ams.org>, and world-known museums, such as <www.metmuseum.org>, <www.lacma.org>, <www.tate.org.uk>, <www.louvre.fr>, and <www.rijksmuseum.nl>. The domain names are not to be used as the only evaluation criteria of Web contents; users need to evaluate Web pages in terms of authority (responsibility, validity) and content, described next, rather than in terms of their domain names alone.

4. Is the site someone's personal page? If so, check for that person's affiliation, credentials, motivation, and currency. Is the person trying to promote and commercialize his or her product, service, or program?

Content

The following are some of the most important questions to ask with regard to Web content:

1. What does the Web page contain?
2. Is the Web page designed for advertising/promotional purposes?
3. Is the information fact, editorial, or personal opinion?
4. Does the Web page offer "further readings," bibliographies, and other useful links?
5. Does the Web page provide contextual information that is important to understand the content?
6. Can you detect any bias (gender, political, ethnic, religious, racial)?
7. Is the use of graphics and sound (images, icons, animation, audio files) relevant to the content? Would you be equally satisfied if you searched the text-only version?
8. Is the date and update frequency given? Is the copyright date easy to determine?
9. Are the links to other sites current and easily accessible?
10. Are appropriate credits given to the sources used in the document?
11. Is the site designed for a specific audience in mind, such as middle school and high school students, parents, teachers, administration, researchers, graduate students, general public?
12. Is the Web page engaging, compelling, and inviting you to come back and stay a long time?
13. Is the Web page open to user contributions and community editing? Examples may be from simple surveys and comments to be completed by users, to their narrative contributions, stories, and oral histories. Other examples may be solicitation open to anyone who wishes to contribute.

Structure, visual design, and interface

Some of the following questions are worth examining with regard to the overall Web site design and usability guidelines:

1. Are the general structure, hot links, and the use of other navigational tools user-friendly?
2. Have you detected any error messages, blind links, "under construction," or outdated sites?
3. Is the layout on the screen well-designed and easy to understand (e.g., well labeled? easy to read? white spaces? jargon free?)

4. Is the page designed in a layered mode, or is just about everything put on the main page?

5. Is the page accessible (e.g., no need to login with ID and passwords, even as quests)?

6. Is the page self-explanatory and understandable?

7. Is the page easy to use and navigate (e.g., go "home," go "back")?

8. Is the page consistent (e.g., naming objects, navigation buttons, overall layout, etc.)?

9. Is the use of color, pictorial symbols, and language appropriate for the targeted audience?

10. Is the page visually appealing?

Search features

1. Are there "help" screens and online tutorials with examples available?

2. Which search modes exist currently? (simple search, advanced search)

3. Does the engine support easy search modification?

4. Are navigational tools self-explanatory?

5. Are the pages sufficiently fast in downloading graphics, animation, audio files?

The following section contains useful Web pages from a wide variety of sources and on different topics. Now that you know how to evaluate Web material, check the pages below in terms of the four types of criteria that we have just introduced: Authority, Content, Structure, and Search Features.

1. URLs of governmental information sources:

The official Web page of the **Library of Congress** contains documents that describe the library and its history, exhibits and events, digital library collections, and more <www.loc.gov> as well as a collection of full-text legislation and major bills at <thomas.loc.gov>.

The American Memory Project at the Library of Congress consists of primary sources and archival materials relating to American culture and history. Most of these offerings are from the Library's special collections <lcweb2.loc.gov/amhome.html>.

U.S. Geological Survey features science topics including those on global warming and protection of coral reefs <www.usgs.gov>. Online maps of the United States are sponsored by the U.S. Bureau of the Census; use its browser to redraw maps with various features such as county lines, highways, parks, water bodies, cities, streets, and census tracks; other features include zoom-in and zoom-out controls <tiger.census.gov>.

U.S. Bureau of the Census publishes an authoritative summary of mainly federally collected statistical data. It is supplemented by Historical Statistics of the U.S., Colonial Times to 1970 <www.census.gov>. Statistical Abstract of the U.S. includes data on population, employment by occupation, personal income, consumer price index, sales by kind of business, U.S. exports and imports <www.census.gov/statab/www>.

CIA World FactBook gives detailed information about worldwide countries <www.cia.gov/library/publications/the-world-factbook/index.html>.

Other Web documents related to **health** and **health statistics** include:

Centers for Disease Control and Prevention <www.cdc.gov>, CDC home page is also available in Spanish. The page contains the *Emerging Infectious Disease Journal* (EID Journal) that tracks trends and analyzes new and reemerging infectious disease issues around the world. You can read information from *Morbidity and Mortality Weekly Report* (MMWR). Of special interest is "Travelers' Health," how to protect yourself from disease when traveling outside the United States.

The mission statement of GirlsHealth <www.girlshealth.gov> says that the Web site, developed by the Office on Women's Health in the Department of Health and Human Services, is "to promote healthy, positive behaviors in girls between the ages of 10 and 16. The site gives girls reliable, useful information on the health issues they will face as they become young women, and tips on handling relationships with family and friends, at school and at home" (accessed April 26, 2007). Among the topics to choose from, there is plenty of information on fitness, nutrition, diseases, drugs, alcohol and smoking (check the 'guess what's in a cigarette?' quiz), bullying, safety, and more. The site gives information for educators, parents and caregivers, and girls ages 10 to 16. The topics of fitness and nutrition, sexuality, emotional health, and more are well covered by the Center for Young Women's Health, created by **Children's Hospital in Boston** <www.youngwomenshealth.org>. Special features include "meet our peers," "online health chats" and "join our e-mail list."

Occupational Safety and Health Administration, OSHA <www.osha.gov>, offers a proposed new ergonomic standard and its new 'Plain Language' workplace poster.

World Health Organization at <www.who.int> is available in multiple languages. You can access WHO reports and other documentation about communicable diseases, disease outbreak news, statistical data, and various health topics.

PubMed at <www.ncbi.nlm.nih.gov/PubMed> is a project developed by the National Center for Biotechnology Information, NCBI, at the National Library of Medicine. PubMed gives you access to bibliographic information in the fields of medicine, nursing, dentistry, veterinary medicine, and health care.

Important Web resources related to presidential debates and **political parties** are at the University of Michigan's site <www.lib.umich.edu/govdocs/psusp.html>. The official Web site of the Democratic National Committee highlights its platform, online polls, debates, campaign trail, and other news from the headquarters <www.democrats.org>. The Republican National Committee homepage offers information on RNC's history, issues, proposals, and debates <www.rnc.org>. You might be interested to read the 1912 Platform of the Progressive Party, also known as the "Bull Moose Party". The Party opposed the conservatism of the regular Republican Party and called for aggressive social legislation. How would you search for background information on this party? For information about the Reform Party, visit <www.reformparty.org>; for the Green Party visit <www.greenparty.org>.

2. URLs of education-related sources (of special interest to teachers, librarians, parents)

Classroom CONNECT <www.classroom.net> offers information for educators, students, parents, and anyone interested in teaching, learning, and information technology.

The Educator's Reference Desk at <www.eduref.org> incorporates more than 2,000 lesson plans, and more than 3,000 links to education resources and education Listserv Archives. The portal may be searched or browsed through broad subject categories, including counseling, educational management, technology, evaluation, family life, reference, teaching, and more.

Examine the following education-related URLs keeping in mind the four evaluation criteria:

KidsClick! <www.kidsclick.org> searches more than 600 topics for kids, such as facts and people, religion and mythology, society and government, literature, sports and recreation, the arts, health and family, science and math, geography, history and biography; click on machines and transportation and visit an annotated list of sources on robots and robotics.

Find out how the Internet Public Library (IPL) <www.ipl.org/div/teen> selects material. The site contains information ranging from homework to career and college, health, math and science, sports, as well as politics and government. At the time of this writing, the site featured the Works of the Bard: Surfing with the Bard, Shakespeare Bookshelf, etc. Special collections contain blogs, literary criticism, and a science fair, as well as searching tools. The IPL's teen space <www.ipl.org/div/teen> has organized links into clubs and organizations, health and sexuality, reading and writing, school and homework help, sports, entertainment, graphic novels guide, and frequently asked embarrassing questions.

Teachers and media specialists will find the following noncommercial Web resources useful:

Web site at <www.ala.org/ICONN/index.html> is an initiative of the American Association of School Librarians (AASL). Excellent sources are organized for students and the entire family. The Young Adults Library Services Association, also known as YALSA, is one of the fastest growing divisions of the American Library Association (ALA). Their TEEN READ WEEK™ Web site at <www.ala.org/teenread> includes annotated lists of recommended reading for teens <www.ala.org/yalsa/booklists>, tips for planning and promoting TEEN READ WEEK events, and links to the Teen's Top Ten.

The U.S. Department of Education home page at <www.ed.gov> gives access to ERIC Digests, technology, National Library of Education, and finding K-12 schools and colleges. It lists contacts, funding opportunities, and more.

California Department of Education at <www.cde.ca.gov> has organized its home page under the following main headings: Curriculum & Instruction; Testing & Accountability; Professional Development; Finance & Grants; Data & Statistics; Learning Support, and Specialized Programs. It highlights the No Child Left Behind Act of 2001, and standardized testing and reporting (STAR).

For **science** programs, go to Mad Scientist Network <www.madsci.org>. In addition, for curriculum resources, visit SCORE Science lessons for high school grade levels <scorescience.humboldt.k12.ca.us>. You can search for lesson plans that have a clear connection to science standards that are problem-based, and specific to your subject matter and grade level. By selecting grade level 10 and genetics, we retrieved excellent lesson plans, also known as WebQuests. "DNA for dinner?" <http://dnafordinner.blogspot.com/> by W. E. Peace, for example, is well linked to a curricular standard that is specific to the 10th grade; the lesson is divided into sections: Introduction, Task, Process, Resources, Evaluation, and Conclusion.

For **math** Web programs, visit Swarthmore Dr. Math <www.forum.swarthmore.edu/> as well as Cornell Gateway <www.tc.cornell.edu/Services/Education/Gateways/Math_and_Science>. The gateway contains links to general topics as well as geometry; fractals; history of math; tables; constants; definitions; funny, irrational pages about Pi and other numbers; and free and commercial software. Also check instructional resources at the SCORE history site <score.kings.k12.ca.us>.

For **social studies** lessons, visit SCORE history site <score.rims.k12.ca.us> and then search for specific grade levels and topics. This author's search for 10th grade social studies lessons (World History and Geography: The Modern World) resulted in lesson plans along with resources and activities.

EXERCISE 7.2: Finding Web documents by knowing URLs

URL-known search: If you know the URL address of an electronic resource on the Web, enter the location. From there, point-and-click on any among the subject headings to see specific Web sites. You can save your Web sites with the bookmark feature (pull down the bookmark menu, and click on add). Some sites are of special importance to parents <www.ala.org/parents/index.html, www.tekmom.com/>, teachers <ericir.syr.edu/>, and media specialists <www.ala.org/ICONN/index.html>. Periodically check INFOEN at <infoen.net> for updates and news.

Internet as a worldwide digital collection

We will navigate and search Hypertext-based resources on the World Wide Web, or Web, by means of using search engines, such as Google and MSN Live; subject guides, such as

Yahoo!, and meta-search engines such as Dogpile and Metacrawler. Here, we introduce only the representative search engines and meta-search engines. See Table 7.3 in the back of this chapter for comparison between Internet search tools.

Search engines

Ask <www.ask.com> combines Teoma and Direct Hit search tools to collect and index Web resources. To get started, use simple queries. Advanced queries use operators such as AND, OR, and NOT; you may ask to get results in a particular language, and within a certain time limit. Searches may be exact phrases, in the title or in the URL. It also allows for ranked matches so that those pages with the highest scores are placed at the head of the retrieved list.

Tips for advanced search are at <www.ask.com/webadvanced/>.

Searching with **Google**. As expected, besides the basic search, you can run advanced searches <www.google.com/advanced_search?hl=en> allowing you to find results with all of the words, with the exact phrases, and with at least one of the words. Furthermore, you can request a specific language, file format, date, and domain, as well as specifics in terms of finding only images, maps, books, video, news, etc.

Compare simple and advanced search results by typing the following two instructions:

Type in: rembrandt (how many entries did you get?)

Type in: rembrandt site:art museum (how many matches did you get now?)

From more than 2.5 million entries, we have reduced them to the most relevant few. Knowing how to use specific search features pays off.

EXERCISE 7.3: Learning from Web documents

To see a collection of some of the best images from NASA's planetary exploration program, enter: pds.jpl.nasa.gov/planets/

Enter EARTH; fill-in the following data:

1. Average distance from Sun:

2. Highest point on the surface:

3. Rotation period (in Earth hours):

4. Revolution period (length of year):

Subject directories and meta-search engines

Subject categories are a convenient way to explore millions of Web sites especially if we are not comfortable with the vocabulary of a given subject matter. Categories are typically arranged alphabetically (see Table 7.1 below) and organized hierarchically. Examples of directories are:

- Librarians' Internet Index <www/lii.org>
- INFOMINE <infomine.ucr.edu>
- Academic Info <www.academicinfo.us>
- Yahoo! <dir.yahoo.com>
- Google <dir.google.com>

Yahoo! <dir.yahoo.com> gives you options to browse its subject directory. The main Yahoo! categories remain the same.

Art and Humanities (literature, photography…)	**News and Media** (TV, papers)
Business and Economy (finance, software…)	**Recreation and Sports** (sports, travel, outdoors)
Computers and Internet (games, software…)	**Reference** (libraries, quotations)
Education (K-12, colleges & universities)	**Regional** (countries, U.S.)
Entertainment (cool links, movies, humor, music)	**Science** (astronomy, engineering)
Government (elections, law, taxes)	**Social Science** (archaeology, economy, language)
Health (medicine, fitness)	**Society and Culture** (people, religion)

Table 7.1: Yahoo!'s main subject categories

Yahoo! has also added New Addition as well as RSS (Real Simple Syndication) for arts, music, sports, and television.

In addition to exploring broad, hierarchically organized categories, you can search topics by typing in keywords. The simple search looks for the keywords in titles and comments, and returns the highest ranking matches. The advanced search <search.yahoo.com/> asks you to fill in the fields in order to return results that are matching your information need more closely. For example, if your topic was biomes, you could specify a desired domain (such as .gov, .edu, .org), language, file format, and other delimiters.

Dogpile <www.dogpile.com> is a meta-search engine that incorporates results of Web pages, images, videos, news, and audio files from engines such as Ask, Google, and Yahoo!. Its advanced search option lets you modify queries in order to give you precise hits.

Webcrawler <webcrawler.com/> is a meta-search engine that uses "Web robot" to harvest results from the most popular search engines (for example, Ask, Google, Yahoo!, LookSmart, Windows Live). Next, it eliminates duplicates from multiple search engines, and presents a list of entries from multimedia files including Web pages, images, video, and music. Webcrawler features searches that change periodically. At the time of this writing, the selected searches include results on the topics of stem cells, funny videos, and swimsuits.

Invisible Web search tools

Not everything is available on the Web. What search engines "uncover" is known as the "visible Web." However, there are millions of pages that are not translated into HTML codes, and therefore are invisible to search engines. Some of the contents may be password protected in online databases, such as ProQuest and JSTOR. For example, GOOGLE SCHOLAR <scholar.google.com>, provides bibliographic citations, and sometimes abstracts to peer reviewed journal contents for which "spiders" and "crawlers" find stable hotlinks (URLs) but do not tap the protected data and information that is accessible only through subscription.

In order to give you a flavor of contents that is generally "hidden" from search engines, we offer descriptions of three different gateways that are available to you. These are Librarians' Internet Index, INFOMINE, and Academic Info, explained next.

Librarians' Internet Index <lii.org> is a publicly funded Web directory and weekly newsletter, "New This Week," featuring high quality sites that are selected, organized, and maintained by librarians. The content includes 14 topics with nearly 300 related subtopics. The topics are arranged alphabetically, ranging from Arts and Humanities, Computers, Health, and Law, to Regions of the World, Science, and Society and Social Science. The content is selected on the basis of the criteria posted and described on the LII Web site; these are:

- Availability
- Credibility
- Authorship
- External links
- Legality

Other important criteria are scope and audience, content, design, functionality, and shelf life.

Basic INFOMINE Searching:
Searches retrieve terms in: 1) title, subject, author, keyword, and description. 2) three or four pages of rich text from the Web site.

Advanced and Subject Category Searching:
Searches are set to retrieve terms in title, subject, author, keyword, and description OR you can select which fields to search.

A search for:	Retrieves:
smog	*smog*
industr*	*industries, industry, industrial, industrialization, ...*
rivers	only the word *rivers*
rivers*	rivers, Riverside, Riverside's, National Scenic Rivers
|rivers|	Only the **exact, complete** term rivers in INFOMINE's subject, title, author, or keyword fields. (rivers **not** Rivers, Joan) Use "pipe" symbol ... usually on the \ key
"new mexico"	new must appear **next to** mexico to get New Mexico in that order
new mexico	new **and** mexico (retrieves Mexico and New Zealand and new fashions in Mexico, as well as New Mexico)
|new mexico|	*New Mexico* retrieves only the **exact, complete** phrase in INFOMINE's subject, title, author, or keyword fields. (retrieves *New Mexico* but does not retrieve *University of New Mexico*) Use "pipe" symbol ... usually on the \ key
genetics databases genetics and databases	*genetics* **and** *databases* The two searches retrieve identical results
windows not microsoft	retrieves *windows* **but** not if the word *microsoft* is present
crime and |states| crime |states|	*states* **rather than** *United States* Finds Web sites about *crime in individual states* **rather than** the many more sites about *crime in the United States nationwide*. The two searches retrieve identical results.
rice or oryza	either *rice* **or** *oryza* or both *rice* **and** *oryza*
sustainable (agriculture or farming)	*sustainable* **and** *agriculture* as well as *sustainable* **and** *farming*
renaissance near4 history	*renaissance* **and** *history* **within four words** of one another (retrieves *history of the Renaissance* and *Renaissance drama as cultural history*) The range for near is: near1 to near20

Table 7.2: Advanced search tips from INFOMINE

INFOMINE <infomine.ucr.edu> was established by the University of California at Riverside, Institute of Museum and Library Services <www.mls.gov>, and Fund for the Improvement of Postsecondary Education (FIPSE) <www.ed.gov> in 1994. The site contains scholarly Internet collections that may not be "discovered" through search engines. Sites like **INFOMINE** are sometimes referred to as "deep Web" or "hidden Web" because the content comes from scholarly sources that are not always retrievable by crawlers and Web robots. Besides browsing nine broad areas, one can search directly using a simple query or advanced search.

The tips in Table 7.2 are copied from **INFOMINE's** home page. Because the tips are representative to search syntax of other search engines and online databases, they are given here, with permission from the Regents of the University of California System, developed and supported by the Library of the University of California Riverside.

Academic Info <www.academicinfo.us> is another college-level educational subject directory containing more than 25,000 hand-picked Web resources, specifically designed for high school and college students. The directory provides information on online degree programs and admission test preparation resources, including SAT, GRE, LSAT, and MCAT. The home page tells us that they also offer "timely news and analysis of critical events including the Iraq War, Afghanistan Reconstruction, Hurricane Katrina recovery, the genocide in the Sudan, and the War on Terrorism." Academic Info also publishes a "What's New" monthly mailing.

In summary, Table 7.3 provides a listing of representative Internet finding tools.

What you have learned

Chapter 7 presents an overview of searching digital libraries focusing on conceptual aspects of searching. This chapter particularly emphasizes a hands-on approach to searching the Internet's search engines.

Equally important is the section on *How to think critically about Web documents*. We list URLs of a wide variety of information sources in different disciplines and then suggest that you explore some of these and evaluate them in terms of evaluation criteria. The following list includes selective terms and some of the concepts that have been introduced in this chapter.

Hypertext Markup Language (HTML)	A subset of standardized general markup languages that is used to create Web documents.
Internet	The collective name for a worldwide network of computer networks using the same telecommunication protocol (TCP/IP for transmission control protocol/Internet protocol) distributed net.

Name	Young adult	Meta-search engine	Search engine
Ask http://www.ask.com/	Ask for Kids http://www.askforkids.com/ The page includes sources for parents as well as human selected sites (as opposed to robot-selected) on various 7-12 grade related topics: Science Math help History, world atlas Biography Clip art		Combines Teoma ("wisdom of the crowds") and Direct Hit (click based ranking) search engines to determine relevancy. Simple, advanced mode. Operators: + and; - not, OR. Search can be narrowed down to title, URL, domain, lang. Search tools allow for searching images, news, maps, blogs, feeds, etc. Natural language query.
Google http://www.google.com	Google directory for kids & teens divides pages into broad categories (arts, games, computers, health, family, international, teen life, etc., with subdivision into "girls only,""sexuality," and "fashion." http://www.google.com/Top/Kids_and_Teens/		Fast, precise, simple search engine offers for web searching as well as for images, video, scholar (http://scholar.google.com), maps, patents, earth, catalogs, and more. Advanced searching lets you find results with all of the words, exact phrase, without certain words, in title, a domain, language; you can ask for alerts on the topic of your choice.
Yahoo! www.yahoo.com	Yahooligans! http://www.yahooligans.com Subject directory for kids organized around themes: "Things you can do," International kids, entertainment, homework help, reference, and more.		Search directory for general public on broad topics including health, real estate, shopping, travel, yellow pages. Health is subdivided into "summer shape up," "women's health,""medical and safety resources," etc. Besides browsing topics, search http://search.yahoo.com topics by means of using keywords (biomes) in a dialog box. Create specific searches by modifying your search to a domain, title, language.
Dogpile http://www.dogpile.com	Kids like it?	Searches several search engines (known as multi-threaded searches)	
Searchenginewatch www.searchenginewatch.com		Excellent multi-threaded engine	
Librarians Internet Index http://www.lii.org/		Lii	16,000+ Web sources, Invisible Web (AKA); basic and advanced search modes; phrase search " " plus AND as implied operator, OR, NOT; * used for stem searching.
Infomine http://infomine.ucr.org/		Infomine	About 120,000 Web sources for college-level students. Advanced search features are in given in Table 7.2.
AcademicInfo http://www.academicinfo.us		AcademicInfo	More than 25,000 Web sources are especially useful for high school and college students.

Table 7.3: Internet finding tools

Microsoft Explorer®	A browser used to access Web documents. See also Netscape Navigator®, below, as well as Mozilla Firefox browser.
Multimedia	An integrated information presentation consisting of text, photographic images, animation, sound files, and video clips in digital form that creates a stand-alone or networked product.
Netscape Navigator	A browser used to access Web documents.
Social Network **Software Tools**	Recently, we have seen a plethora of "social network software" tools. Some examples include podcasting, RSS, blogging, wiki spaces, and emerging innovative Web 2.0 applications.
URL	Uniform Resource Locator that allows a standardized form of addressing the location of Web documents on the Internet.
Worldwide Web (WWW)	A graphic Hypertext-based system for finding and accessing Web resources via hot links and buttons. Many Web pages are "uncovered" by crawlers and search engines; however, millions of published documents that appear in peer-reviewed journals are only accessible through password protected online databases, hence known as "invisible" Web, also known as deep Web.

Think Guide 4   Evaluation of Web Sources

How to think critically about Web documents

Because not all Web documents are equally well suited and valuable, this section summarizes main types of criteria that you could use to evaluate the material produced on the Web. These criteria are authority and content. Under each of these two headings, we suggest questions that will help you to evaluate Web documents.

Authority

- Is the creator/author/producer of the Web page given? Is there a distinction made between the author of the content, the Webmaster, and the contact person?

- If the author, editor, or creator of the intellectual content of the Web page is given, are links included to their credentials and affiliations? This is important because it gives you an opportunity to get in touch with the author in order to obtain more detailed information, explanation, and further clarification on various issues. Furthermore, knowing the authors' names, you can explore work that may not be available through search engines. Is the site someone's personal page? If so, check for person's affiliation, credentials, motivation, and currency. Is the person trying to promote and commercialize his or her product, service, or program?

Content

- What does the Web page contain?
- Is the Web page designed for advertising/promotional purposes?
- Is the information fact, editorial, or personal opinion?
- Does the Web page offer "further readings," bibliographies, and other useful links?
- Does the Web page provide contextual information that is important to understand the content?
- Can you detect any bias (gender, political, ethnic)?
- Is the use of graphics (e.g., images, icons, animation) relevant to the content? Would you be equally satisfied if you searched the text-only mode?
- Is the date and update frequency given?
- Is the copyright date easy to determine?
- Are the links to other sites current and easily accessible?
- Are appropriate credits given to the sources used in the document?

- Is the site designed for a specific audience in mind, such as high school students, parents, teachers, researchers, graduate students, general public?
- Is the Web page engaging, compelling, and inviting you to revisit?
- Is the Web page open to user contributions and community editing?

CHAPTER 8

Finding Magazine and Newspaper Articles

In this chapter, you will learn how to:

- Find articles in magazines, journals, and newspapers
- Distinguish popular magazines from scholarly journals
- Use different search strategies for different information needs

This chapter will introduce you to the various ways of finding information in periodical literature such as magazines and newspaper articles. The term periodical means any publication that is issued continually. Periodicity varies; some periodicals, like dailies, come out each day, such as the *Washington Post* <www.washingtonpost.com/>, and the *Los Angeles Times* <www.latimes.com>; some are issued weekly, like *Newsweek*; others are published monthly, four times a year, and so forth. Instead of scanning through issues of hundreds of individual magazines, newspapers, and journals, many people typically use magazine databases, also known as periodical indexes. Just as library catalogs give you access to book-like materials, online magazine databases provide access to individual articles in magazines and newspapers. These databases are designed to save you time and to make your library research easy and effective. Examples of online databases are ProQuest <proquest.com/pqdweb>, EBSCOhost <search.epnet.com/login.asp>, InfoTrac <infotrac.galegroup.com/itweb>, JSTOR <www.jstor.org>, and SIRS

<sks.sirs.com>. Increasingly, online databases offer full length articles. In addition to predominantly text oriented databases, ARTstor <www.artstor.org> contains images from numerous worldwide art collections that can be downloaded, manipulated, and incorporated in students' projects and classroom settings. Access to all these databases is password protected.

What are the differences between contents from these databases just listed and others obtained via "Googling?" How are issues regarding intellectual property related to using the contents from commercial databases (e.g., ProQuest, JSTOR) versus the contents obtained from search engines? Is most of the published information now becoming available free of charge on the Web? I've read somewhere that Google Print Project is going to digitize the entire world's published knowledge. Are all these databases necessary to use in one's research? How do I decide which ones to use first? Answers to these and other questions will be found shortly, all in this chapter.

Introduction to online databases

Online databases such as ProQuest are bibliographic services that provide access to articles in magazines, journals, and newspapers by title, subject, author, and often other access points. This database provides access to both scholarly and popular articles. These are defined next.

Scholarly articles are peer-reviewed by experts in a given field for validity, originality, clarity, completeness, and bibliographic honesty. The articles are signed, bibliographies are extensive, and articles appear in journals that are published by academic and scientific societies. Examples are the *American Film, American History, American Scientist, Nature, Scientific American,* and the *Journal of Applied Physics*. On the other hand, **popular magazines** feature extensive advertisements of commercial products and services, and their articles of popular content are often written by journalists and staff writers. The articles are current, often not signed, and typically have no cited references at the end of the articles.

> NOTE: Online databases, such as ARTstor, InfoTrac, JSTOR, ProQuest, and SIRS, to mention just a few, do not show the location of items in individual libraries. In our example, "Mapping the cancer genome," you would either find the article in the March issue (2007) of *Scientific American* in your local library, or request the article electronically. Alternatively, your library can borrow an item from another library through a service known as an interlibrary loan.

The following are examples of topics that are suitable for periodical literature:

- Someone has told me of a recent cover story that appeared in *U.S. News & World Report*; the article discusses supply of water, access to clean water, conservation issues, as well as basic facts and figures.

- Are there any stories on the Tiananmen Square Massacre, especially from the perspective of historians outside of the United States? For example, what do Japanese sinologists say about the incident that took place in Spring of 1989?

- Is there research on attitudes toward injury risks? Specifically, you are interested in the use of helmets in the prevention of motorcycle accidents.

- Are there any current scholarly articles that discuss the presence of methane on Mars and Titan?

Of special importance is a checklist for contacts and summaries of several online databases that were introduced in this chapter (see Appendix L).

Your library may be subscribing to several online databases such as EBSCOhost, InfoTrac, JSTOR, or ProQuest. They are comparable in some respects and certain search features apply to all. For example, many articles are available in full-length. They are password protected. The contents are searchable by means of using a simple search and more advanced techniques. They use "Boolean operators" that we introduced in Chapter 3. There are also important differences among these services, and you need to know which database would be the first best choice for you and your projects. It pays off to be familiar with the contents of various databases. They may offer the same interface, that is to say, a similar look and feel, to very different contents, services, and programs. For example, ProQuest Information and Learning has recently added to its original core the following online databases: CultureGrams <online.culturegrams.com>, eLibrary, and SIRS (containing, for example, SIRS Researcher, SIRS Renaissance, and SIRS Government Reporter). This means that you will have the same type of interface for all these different services offered from a single provider.

Examples of searching from ProQuest

Now we want to show you how to effectively search **ProQuest** <proquest.umi.com>. Your library may have already bookmarked ProQuest for you so you can use it to connect directly next time. It gives comprehensive access to magazine articles. There are several ways to search ProQuest:

- **Searching by topic** lets you select articles from broad topics
- **Searching by word** offers the **basic** and the **advanced** techniques
- **Searching for publication** allows you to look for specific issues of a magazine

The easiest way to familiarize yourself with the ProQuest online database is to select the "searching by topic" option. You can enter a topic in a dialog box or browse any of the 11 broad topics from the following main menu:

Arts & Humanities	Lifestyles & Culture
Business & Industry	Politics, Government, & Law
Computers & Internet	Science & Mathematics
Economics & Trade	Social Issues & Policy
Education	Sports & Entertainment
Environmental Health	

Figure 8.1: Searching by topic in ProQuest

If you are looking for articles on **acid rain**, you might start off by exploring the environment as a topic. It is subdivided into more specific topics, such as natural resources, nature, and pollution, which in turn will show you even further subdivisions: pollutants, pollution control, and types of pollution; narrower topics, such as acid rain, air pollution, noise pollution, and water pollution will contain numerous articles that you can selectively print or e-mail to your account.

EXERCISE 8.1: Topical search

Using the Topic Search option, find information on acid rain in the Niger Delta. Cite one of the articles you found in the space below (see Chapter 9 on how to cite):

Using your browser's BACK button, go to the main menu and explore other topics. Alternatively, you may want to click on the NEW SEARCH arrow in the upper left corner to initiate a new search.

EXERCISE 8.2: Selecting the closest heading

Suppose you decide to switch your interest to finding articles about the Cold War. Which general topic would you choose? Look at the 11 topics in figure 8.1. How many "clicks" do you have to make before you find articles on your topic?

Searching by word using the basic or advanced techniques is another approach to finding articles in ProQuest. The screen on page 105 shows you a keyword search using the advanced search mode for articles on the Tiananmen Square Massacre. You can request peer-reviewed articles as full-texts.

For a tutorial on search tips, go to <http://proquest.umi.com/i-std/en/pri/advanced/adv.htm>.

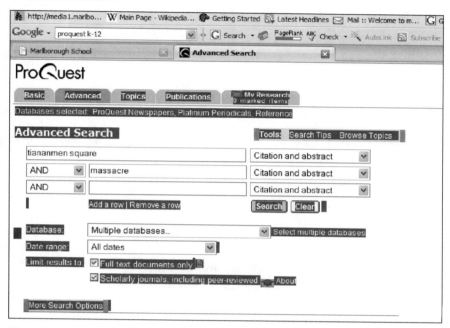

Figure 8.2: Advanced mode of searching the ProQuest database

The third way to search ProQuest is to do a **search on publications**. It requires little or no typing of search terms; all you have to do is to click on list publications to view an alphabetical listing of hundreds of magazine titles, journals, and newspapers that are included in ProQuest. If you know the title of a magazine, you can type it into the appropriate search box (adolescence; addictive behaviors). As of this writing, there are 2,366 magazine titles, newspapers, and other periodicals in the ProQuest database. Approximately 43 percent (n=1,040) of these titles offer full-text articles in their volumes. Another important piece is to know that different periodicals vary in terms of their coverage. Some go back more than 10 years; others, like *Addiction*, cover a period between 1997 and 2000.

ProQuest gives several options so that you can specify your search by time (current articles or from back files); by type of articles (from newspapers, magazines, reference books); and by search source (from citations and abstracts to full-texts with graphics).

Using **Search by Word-Basic**, find articles on energy. Click on the Subject list link to view narrower subjects of the term "energy." Write down these more specific terms.

Notice the different ways you can modify your search. Use some of these pull-down menus to search back files (2003-2007), or to restrict your search to full-text peer-reviewed articles only.

EXERCISE 8.3: Publication search

1. Click on list publications and visit *America's Civil War*. What is the latest issue of this magazine (volume, issue, and date)?

2. Now select the September issue (vol 12, issue 4, 1999) and find an article by Roy Morris, Jr. What does the image show for the article?

3. Find the cover story by Kenneth Terrell in the *U.S. News and World Report* (July 2, 2007) on Civil War. What are some of the surprising findings that primary sources illuminated and explained about the American Civil War?

4. Go back to the magazine titles and select *Civil War History*. Read about primary sources on women nurses in the Civil War (vol 45, issue 2, 1999). Who wrote these stories?

5. Look up *Technology Review* young innovators with the year's best ideas. Check out the September/October issue (volume 109, number 4) of 2006 and read about TR35 researchers involved in cleaning toxic waste with nano-particles, tagging the Web, inventing plastic semi-conductors, user authentication, and security functions.

> 1. Global Warming: Are Environmentalists Part of the Problem?
> Robert W Kates. Environment. Washington: Jan/Feb 2007. Vol. 49, Iss. 1; p. 0_2 (1 page)
> 📄 Full text   📄 Full Text - PDF   📄 Abstract
>
> 2. Cyber-Community for Housing, Consumer Economics Created
> Kelly Shannon Manley, Anne L Sweaney. Journal of Family and Consumer Sciences. Alexandria: Jan 2007. Vol. 99, Iss. 1; p. 41 (2 pages)
> 📄 Full text   📄 Full Text - PDF   📄 Abstract
>
> 3. Green Plants, Fossil Fuels, and Now Biofuels
> David Pimentel, Tad Patzek. Bioscience. Washington: Nov 2006. Vol. 56, Iss. 11; p. 875 (1 page)
> 📄 Full text   📄 Full Text - PDF   📄 Abstract
>
> 4. PUTTING ENERGY EFFICIENCY IN A SUSTAINABILITY CONTEXT: THE COLD FACTS ABOUT REFRIGERATORS
> Jack N Barkenbus. Environment. Washington: Oct 2006. Vol. 48, Iss. 8; p. 11 (11 pages)
> 📄 Full text   📄 Full Text - PDF   📄 Abstract
>
> 5. Sustainable Consumption
> Timothy O'Riordan. Environment. Washington: Oct 2006. Vol. 48, Iss. 8; p. 0_2 (1 page)
> 📄 Full text   📄 Full Text - PDF   📄 Abstract

Figure 8.3: Result of a ProQuest search on energy conservation

The **Search by Word-Advanced** option lets you run more sophisticated searches than the basic option. Take this opportunity to look at other qualifiers in the same pull-down menu; for example, you can ask to see a specific image of Cordoba (Spain) if your search is qualified by the "image caption." Other ways to limit your search are: abstract, title, author, geographic name, company or organization, image caption, and subject. This feature will make your search precise and effective.

EXERCISE 8.4: Narrowing down your search results

Find the most current articles that discuss **energy conservation**. Use some of the limit features that we have just discussed. Write down your search plan in the space below:

Consider the following topics and start off by KEYWORD searching.

Topics in social studies that are suitable for online magazine databases are: affirmative action; capital punishment; future of newspapers in digital age; role of women in Afghanistan (country of your choice); contributions of persons such as Albert Einstein, Duke Ellington, Tiger Woods, and Jane Addams to the American culture.

Topics in science that are suitable for online magazine databases are: regulation of air, water, soil and oil pollution; greenhouse effect; acid rain in specific countries; renewable resources; stem cell research; cleaner diesel engines; genetic engineering.

SIRS <sks.sirs.com> is an editorially selected source including (i) Researcher (see Figure 8.4), (ii) Government Reports, and (iii) Renaissance.

EXERCISE 8.5: Publication search

Using the advanced option, search for articles about Islam in Spain. Qualify the word Spain to the "location" field and use the AND operator between these two terms.

1. How many articles did you get that match your request?

2. Which among the first 10 articles contain text and graphics?

Bonus Questions:

3. How many articles are there on the American Civil War that contain illustrations?

4. Could you find anything that contains illustrations about Christmas during the American Civil War?

Figure 8.4: SIRS Researcher interface with "Your 'Top 10'" controversial issues

In addition to keyword search and subject heading search in the basic and advanced modes, SIRS offers special features, including a "spotlight" article as well as "Your 'TOP 10'" topics. The 'TOP 10' SIRS Researcher leading issues at the time of this writing (June 7, 2007), are displayed in Figure 8.5.

TOPIC (number of all resources on the topic)	TOPIC (number of all resources on the topics)
Global warming (513)	Teenage pregnancy (143)
Marijuana legalization (192)	Gun control (224)
Capital punishment (403)	Abortion (237)
Gangs (192)	School violence (280)
Immigration (513)	Child abuse (170)

Figure 8.5: SIRS Researcher 'TOP Leading Issues'

Each of the 10 topics is treated uniformly starting with an overview, "my Analysis," suggested keywords, as well as "see also" subject headings that would lead one to related articles on the same topic. All resources are divided into specific formats including newspapers, magazines, government reports, primary sources, viewpoints, reference sources, graphics, and Web selected sites.

For example, the topic "Global Warming," with 513 resources, can be "dissected" into specific newspaper articles (201), magazine articles (165), reports (77), primary sources (7), viewpoints (35), two references, 233 pictures, and 74 Web editorially selected sites. Among the magazine articles is one titled *"Black Water Rising,"* displayed below (Figure 8.6).

(an icon saying that graphics are included in the article)

World Watch Vol. 19, No. 5 Sept./Oct. 2006; Lexile Score: <u>1410</u>; 24K, SIRS Researcher **Summary:** "The coastal parishes of Louisiana are sinking, on average, about 11 millimeters each year. At the same time, global sea level has been slowly rising over the last century, at 1.0-2.5 millimeters per year. The two trends have consigned half a million hectares of South Louisiana to the sea since 1932; the ongoing rate is about one and a half football fields every hour. Much of the lost land was coastal wetlands, which historically protected New Orleans by slowing and soaking up storm surges (the sudden rises in sea level that occur as hurricanes come ashore). The remaining wetlands are increasingly fragile, fragmented by canals built for navigation and access to the area's oil and gas. All these factors make New Orleans particularly vulnerable to hurricanes, but within a few decades many more low-lying coastal areas around the world may be equally threatened." *(World Watch)* This article examines the "growing global threat of rising seas and bigger hurricanes." **Descriptors:** <u>Global temperature changes</u>, <u>Climatic changes</u>, <u>Coast changes</u>, <u>Ocean temperature</u>, <u>Long-range weather forecasting</u>, <u>Arctic regions</u>, <u>Climate</u>, <u>Sea level</u>, <u>Sea ice</u>, <u>Hurricanes</u>, <u>Forecasting</u>, <u>Antarctica</u>, <u>Climate</u>, <u>Greenland</u>, <u>Global warming</u>

Figure 8.6: An entry from SIRS Researcher on "Global Warming" from 'TOP 10'

Examples of searching from EBSCOhost®

EBSCOhost <epnet.com> provides about 250 full-text and annotated resources covering a wide range of topics from Arts and Media, English and Language Arts, Current Issues, to Health, Math and Science, Social Studies, Sports, and Technology. Special features such as Top Searches, Spotlight Topic, and Teacher Resources add a special value to the expected search elements. Basic and advanced searching, as well as a variety of search limits that help you sharpen your search requirement, are offered. For example, this author's search for harlem renaissance in English and Language Arts showed a listing of possible headings that are applicable to my search (e.g., Authors, Literary Criticism, Plays, Poetry, World Literature, and Writing).

A health related topic on eating disorders among teens was searched as follows:

eating disorders AND (teen* or adolescent*) produced numerous results, further limited by using several qualifiers, such as time (2000 to 2007), full text peer reviewed articles only, for a certain grade level, and from particular type of resources (e.g., magazines, reports, primary sources, photos).

Examples from JSTOR

JSTOR is non-profit organization offering high resolution scanned articles from core scholarly journals, many of which date as far back as the 1600s. From JSTOR's mission statement <www.jstor.org/about/mission.html>, their goal is to:

- Build a reliable and comprehensive archive of important scholarly journal literature.

- Improve dramatically access to these journals.

- Help fill gaps in existing library collections of journal backfiles.

- Address preservation issues such as mutilated pages and long-term deterioration of paper copy.

- Reduce long-term capital and operating costs of libraries associated with the storage and care of journal collections.

- Assist scholarly associations and publishers in making the transition to electronic modes of publication.

- Study the impact of providing electronic access on the use of these scholarly materials.

There are two basic modes of searching the JSTOR database: by means of browsing disciplines ranging from African-American Studies and Aquatic Sciences to Zoology; and direct searching by means of typing in keywords, authors' names and title words. For example, clicking on African-American Studies, one sees the source periodical titles along with their coverage, including

African American Review 1992-2003, Black American Literature Forum 1976-1991, Negro American Literature Forum 1967-1976, Callaloo 1976-2001 (plus links to recent content 2002-2006), *Journal of African-American History 2002-2003, Journal of Negro History 1916-2001, Journal of Black Studies 1970-2003, Journal of Blacks in Higher Education 1993-2004, Journal of Negro Education 1932-2003, Phylon 1960-2001, Phylon Quarterly 1957-1959, Phylon 1940-1956, Transition 1961-1999* (plus links to recent content 2000-2001).

Searching, both in basic and advanced modes, allows the user to move from being a novice to a sophisticated researcher. "Help" screens and online tutorials are a click away with relevant examples from a variety of disciplines <www.jstor.org/help/search.html>.

While the basic search requires little initial learning, searching by various fields would be helpful for someone who wishes a higher level of specificity. For example, my search for articles on fiction related to gender and sexuality resulted in the following search strategy: (novel& OR fiction) AND feminis* AND (gender OR sexuality).

You will recognize the Boolean operators, AND and OR in the above query. All terms in each of the boxes will be ORed (e.g., novel OR novels OR fiction). Boolean operators are sometimes represented differently, and the best way is to read online search tips before searching. Conceptually, this query could be represented as follows:

Figure 8.7: An example of a search strategy

An ampersand (&) at the end of novel allows for searching both singular and plural forms. An asterisk (*) in feminis allows for searching multiple characters, such as feminism or feminists.

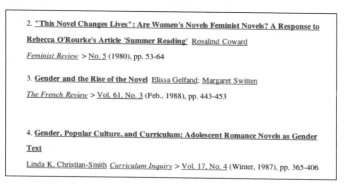

Figure 8.8: A partial result of articles from JSTOR as a result of the above query

One of the image databases, **ARTstor** <www.artstor.org/info/>, contains approximately 300,000 digital images classified and described (see Figure 8.9

below); an additional 5,000 images will be added every three months for the next few years. Each image is fully described and contextualized along with digital rights management information. Descriptive information associated with each image, called metadata, provides data about respective images.

Some of the collections in the database resulted from collaborations with individual photographers (e.g., Larry Qualls), academic institutions (Columbia University), museums, or partnerships with photo archives. Students, teachers, and scholars are finding innovative ways to incorporate high resolution images into their lessons and research projects.

Figure 8.9: Digital image with metadata about the image, all from the ARTstor database

Several ARTstor features paid off. Images can be downloaded, annotated, stored in labeled folders, inserted in presentations, and manipulated in a variety of ways. In addition, students learn to use information regardless of its nature (e.g., textual, graphical) ethically and responsibly. They also learn to give credit not only to printed textual sources, but also to all other artistic expressions such as digital images. In terms of information organization, students learn about information structures, database principles, and information retrieval concepts. For example, students create their folders, label and save folders, give appropriate credits, and simultaneously learn information literacy as well as visual literacy skills in the context of their projects.

Indexes to collections of poems, short stories, and songs

Access to parts of books, such as chapters, individual short stories, poems, and plays are cited below.

- Kale, Tessa, ed. *The Columbia Granger's Index to Poetry in Anthologies*. 13th rev. ed. New York: Columbia University Press, 2006.
- *Short Story Index*. New York: H. W. Wilson, 1953- . Annual.
- Sears, Minnie E. *Song Index*. [n. p.] Shoe String Press, 1966.
- *Play Index*. New York: H. W. Wilson, 1952- . Irregular.

Indexes to historical newspapers online

Anyone interested in studying 19th and 20th century history will find *Historical Newspaper Online* a fascinating and indispensable research tool. You can access password-based Chadwyck-Healey *Historical Newspapers*. As the Introduction says, "You will find the full text of articles illustrating British attitudes towards the United States in the early 1800's and then find references to articles dealing with American reactions to British events in the 20th century. You can trace the development of technology from the power loom to the space shuttle or the end of slavery and the enfranchisement of women." *Historical Newspapers Online* <historynews.chadwyck.com/> provides access to primary sources through the *Palmer's Index to The Times, 1790-1905,* with *Palmer's Full Text Online, 1785-1870; The Official Index to The Times, 1906-1980;* and *Historical Index to The New York Times, 1851-1922. The Making of America* funded by the Andrew W. Mellon Foundation, is a digital library federated project that scanned numerous books, periodical articles, and primary sources in American social history from the antebellum period through Reconstruction. These are available through various digital libraries: University of Michigan <moa.umdl.umich.edu>, Cornell University <cdl.library.cornell.edu/moa>, and others. California Digital Library <www.cdlib.org> also offers free of charge access to some of the historical newspapers. Here's how: from Calisphere <www.calisphere.universityofcalifornia.edu>, search newspaper; you will retrieve nearly 3,000 texts, more than 700 images, and Web sites as well. Then, search within these results; for example, type in San Francisco fire, and your search will result in documents that include the fire in the newspapers that covered the event.

Putting it all together (especially important for instructors)

In order to become a successful researcher, we need to account for a general framework that will help both the students and instructors achieve their common goal: to make students' understanding more applicable, effective, and enjoyable. This framework is captured in three sets of standards:

- National Council for the Social Studies (NCSS) Thematic Strands <www.ncss.org> and National Science Education Standards (NSES) in addition to standards in various disciplines <www.nap.edu/readingroom/books/nses>

- American Association of School Librarians *Standards for the 21st-Century Learner* (2007) <http://www.ala.org/ala/aasl/aaslproftools/learningstandards/standards.cfm>.

- International Society for Technology in Education (ISTE) National Educational Technology Standards for Students NETS-S <www.iste.org> has issued its National Educational Technology Standards for Students: The Next Generation "What students should know and be able to do to learn effectively and live productively in an increasingly digital world ..." <cnets.iste.org/students/pdf/nets_for_students_2007.pdf>.

Thematic strands in the social studies (see page 114) can be used to organize research projects in social study classes; however, not all strands are necessary in all projects. One might emphasize Time, Continuity, and Change (strand ii) as well as Global Connectedness (strand ix), and Science, Technology, and Society (strand viii).

i. Culture

ii. Time, Continuity, and Change

iii. People, Places, and Environment

iv. Individual Development and Identity

v. Individuals, Groups, and Institutions

vi. Power, Authority, and Governance

vii. Production, Distribution, and Consumption

viii. Science, Technology, and Society

ix. Global Connectedness

x. Civic Ideals and Practices

The same project may focus on NETS-S technology productivity tools. Yet, some of the most important lifelong learning skills will come from Information Literacy Standards, including those that pertain to information seeking and access, critical thinking skills, ethical and responsible use of information, and independent learning skills. Regardless of the disciplinary nature, these lifelong learning skills would prepare learners to acquire knowledge effectively, solve problems productively, share their knowledge ethically, and self reflect on their learning experiences.

We started off our discussion in the preface of this book with the five components of learning: content understanding, problem solving, self-reflection, collaboration, and communication. Now, with the *Standards for the 21st-Century Learner* (AASL, 2007), these five components are well represented. See **Think Guide #5** for details on critical thinking.

What you have learned

Some of the key points to remember about online magazine databases, or periodical indexes include:

- What sort of reference sources online magazine databases or periodical indexes are
- What sort of questions are most suitable for online magazine databases
- Main approaches in searching online magazine databases (examples from ProQuest)

This chapter has introduced the following terms and concepts:

Metadata	Description about data; for example, a painting might be described in terms of its fields such as creator's name (e.g., Charles P. Polk), title of work, genre (e.g., portrait, still life, landscape), medium (e.g., oil on canvas, metal), period, collection and provenance (e.g., SFMOMA), size, quality, digital rights management, availability, topic, etc.
Online database	Bibliographic source that provides access to online articles in journals, magazines, and newspapers (e.g., EBSCOhost,

InfoTrac, JSTOR, ProQuest). Recently, we have seen online databases that are full text with graphical material, as well as image databases such as ARTstor. There are many other types of databases that are basically numeric and statistical in nature.

Periodical or serial publications

A publication in any medium issued in successive parts bearing numeric or chronological designations and intended to be continued indefinitely (e.g., newspapers, yearbooks, magazines).

Popular articles

Popular magazines feature extensive advertisements of commercial products and services, and articles of popular content, often written by journalists and staff writers. The articles are current and often not signed.

Scholarly articles

Scholarly articles are peer-reviewed by experts in a given field for validity, originality, clarity, completeness, and bibliographic honesty. The articles are signed, bibliographies are extensive, and articles appear in journals that are published by academic and scientific societies. Examples are the *American Scientist*, *Nature*, *Scientific American*, and the *Journal of Applied Physics*.

Think Guide 5 Working with Articles

How to think critically about magazine and newspaper articles

A healthy dose of skepticism helps while reading articles. Think Guide #5 suggests a number of useful seed questions to keep in mind while reading periodical articles. The word "seed" means that these are not the only questions to ask.

For example, we need to understand questions that a given article raises, evidence and methods used to study given questions, conclusions derived as a result of studying the data and applying certain research techniques, as well as authors' insights; readers' own questions prompted by the article are also important.

Questions raised in the article (main 2-3 ideas):	Evidence used by the author(s) of the article to study the questions:
What was the purpose of the article?	Opinions (author's insights, points of view):
Who is the intended reader of the article? (also, unintended reader)	Any bias detected (political, religious, racial):
Your own questions, inspired by the article:	How would you study/find answer to the questions you raised? How would you study the question differently?

CHAPTER

Citing in Style and Summarizing

In this chapter, you will learn how:

- To cite sources you use in your work regardless of format (book, atlas, cartoon, music) or medium (paper, Web) in order to give credit to others' writings or ideas

- To summarize a work

Understanding how to cite and summarize sources is both critical and basic to all types of research activities. In this chapter you will learn how to give credit to the sources you use in your reports so that readers can examine the evidence you present. To do that we will be using bibliographic citations that give detailed information about materials used in your reports. We define a **bibliographic citation** as a record in precise and consistent form that gives details about an item used in your work.

Chapter 9 will also teach you how to summarize sources that you use in your writing. To **summarize** means to critically analyze sources with regard to their content and presentation. Finally, we will review new terms at the end of this chapter.

Why is citing important?

First, it gives you the evidence to back up what you have said in your writing. Secondly, it helps the reader find an item that was used in your paper. If you must select a writing among several choices, cite the one that is published (rather than unpublished), peer-reviewed, such as a journal article rather than a newspaper article, and written or created by a well-known author/artist or institution rather than by a kindergarten-level student. Failure to give credit to the works and ideas of others' is called **plagiarism**. For details on the topic of plagiarism, readers are referred to Ercegovac (2005) and Ercegovac & Richardson (2004). *Webster's II New Riverside University Dictionary* (1984) defines plagiarism as follows: "**1**. To steal and use (the ideas or writing of another) as one's own. **2**. To take passages or ideas from and use them as one's own." (p. 898).

An article *New Frontiers in Cheating* defines plagiarism as the "act of claiming to be the author of material that someone else actually wrote." The piece goes on to say that "students have plagiarized book reports, term papers, essays, projects, and graduate-degree theses. Teachers—including college professors—have plagiarized journal articles, course materials, and textbooks. Researchers have plagiarized reports, articles, and book chapters. Although academic plagiarism is not new, what is new since the latter years of the 20th century is the ease with which writings on virtually any topic can be misappropriated with little risk of detection. The principal instrument responsible for the recent rapid rise in academic plagiarism has been the Internet, which John Barrie, a developer of software for detecting Web plagiarism, called "a 1.5 billion-page searchable, cut-and-paste encyclopedia." (*Encyclopedia Britannica Online*, 2007).

In a recent story, "Austen scam exposes publishers' pride and prejudice" (*The Guardian*, July 19, 2007), Lassman, head of the Jane Austen Festival in Bath, England, sent manuscripts to 18 editors seeking a publishing contract, using only a slightly disguised language from the well-known novelist. Surprisingly, only one editor, Jonathan Cape, spotted blatant plagiarism between the submitted texts and Austen's *Pride and Prejudice*.

Whether you use a book, a sound recording, or any other source of information in your report, you need to give credit to each source. Information and ideas that you obtain from electronic mail, discussion lists, and Internet sites should also be cited. The following example is a citation of the **book** by Benjamin Franklin, titled *Autobiography and Other Writings*. The book was published in New York by Penguin Books in 1986.

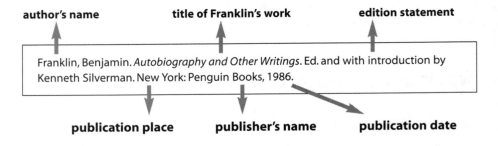

author's name   title of Franklin's work   edition statement

Franklin, Benjamin. *Autobiography and Other Writings*. Ed. and with introduction by Kenneth Silverman. New York: Penguin Books, 1986.

publication place   publisher's name   publication date

A typical bibliographic citation of a **journal article** consists of similar data elements: (a) the authors' names; (b) the complete title of the article; (c) the title of the journal in which the article appeared; (d) the volume, issue, publication date, and pagination. We cite these two items by using a set of rules given by one of the bibliographic style manuals, described shortly.

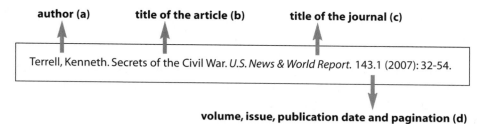

Typically, all sources that you use in reports may be classified as those that are communicated **formally** (books, journal papers, and maps) or **informally** (face-to-face communication and messages obtained via fax, phone, or e-mail).

Sources may also be of archival, primary, and secondary nature.

Archival sources, such as unique, rare, and notable materials, document knowledge, experience, and activities contributing to the human memory. Examples include personal papers and cultural heritage objects, prints and drawings, photographs, maps, coins, rare editions, uniforms, weapons, period furniture, tools, and toys; some of these sources have been digitized, organized, described, preserved, and made accessible through programs such as the *Making of America* at <memory.loc.gov/ndlpcoop/moahtml/ncphome.html>, Cornell University at <cdl.cornell.edu/moa>, and the University of Michigan, <moa.umdl.umich.edu>. For more details, see Think Guide #6.

Primary sources, such as creative and technical writings, or pieces of visual art and music, often draw on information contained in archival sources (e.g., manuscripts, prints, diaries, log books, collections of artifacts from a fieldwork, and laboratory experiments). All primary sources are original in content, methods, ideas, and general techniques they use in their works. An example of a primary source is the content of a book that did not exist before you wrote and published it. Another example may be a doctoral dissertation, or a report that describes an engineering invention or program.

Secondary sources are analyses by scholars who use primary source data, writings, and events in order to discuss or explain certain issues and phenomena. Examples of secondary sources are textbooks, monographs, compendia, anthologies, and other materials that draw on primary sources. In order to access all these sources, we use catalogs and bibliographies that allow you to rapidly locate primary, secondary, and archival sources of information. Examples include your own school library catalog, and remote library catalogs, such as Harvard's at <hollis.harvard.edu>, and

Getty's at <opac.pub.getty.edu>; other examples are bibliographies (*Books in Print*), and online magazine databases (EBSCOhost, JSTOR, ProQuest, SIRS).

The best sources for citing are:

- The item itself (e.g., title page of a book, or an entire item like a map or a video-tape with its container)
- A library catalog for finding books, DVDs, CDs, reports, and atlases
- The bibliography of an item you have used

The sources just outlined give the most complete and accurate information for citing. In order to save time, whenever you use a source, make a complete and accurate citation of that source. This means that while you have an item, write down information about that item fully and accurately. If the item is a book, use information from both sides of the title page; copy the call number, the library that has the book (your school library, public library), and the way you searched and located the item in the library. Write down this information on large reference cards, or enter it directly into your computer files. Use the other side of the reference card for writing a brief summary of the item you used in your work.

Bibliographic style manuals

There are several widely used bibliographic style manuals that can assist you in properly citing the works that you have used in your writing. The following is a partial list of these manuals.

- Gibaldi, Joseph. *MLA Handbook for Writers of Research Papers*. 6th ed. New York: Modern Language Association of America 2003.
- Turabian, K. L. *A Manual for Writers of Term Papers, Theses, and Dissertations: Chicago Style for Students and Researchers*. Rev. by Wayne C. Booth, et al. 7th ed. Chicago: University of Chicago Press, 2007.

How do you decide which style manual to use in your report? This is a matter of tradition, taste, and departmental and personal preferences in your school and among your teachers. It is important to remember that there are no bad styles. However, whichever bibliographic style you use for your bibliographies, follow its rules consistently and rigorously. For the purposes of introducing you to citing and making bibliographies, we will use the *Manual* (Turabian, 2007).

There are commercial citation software management programs for different bibliographic formats. Below, we have given a brief description of widely used programs, especially relevant for those students transitioning from high schools to colleges.

- EndNote® (by Thomson Scientific, <www.endnote.com>) is a reference database manager that specializes in storing, managing, and searching for bibliographic references in your private reference library. It is also a bibliography maker—it automatically builds lists of cited works from word processing documents for in-text citations to compile a bibliography in many formats, including those cited earlier. Other bibliographic software manager applications are Procite® <www.procite.com> and Reference Manager® <www.refman.com>. A fairly recent newcomer, Zotero <www.zotero.org>, is free, easy-to-use, and has been widely popular among college users. It is designed to help you collect, manage, cite, and describe research sources using your own vocabulary.

Choice for a particular manual will vary and depend on personal preference, school's tradition, and many other factors. The following sections will show you how to cite different types of topical sources using the *Manual* (Turabian, 2007). We will take you through a series of seven cases; each case deals with a particular type of source that you may wish to cite in your writing (e.g., a book, an article, a Web site). While you can go directly to these individual cases and corresponding templates, we suggest that you follow the rules from the *Manual*; first, it is not possible to account for all possible cases that you might encounter in your reading and citing; second, the process of citing becomes less mechanical. However, we have attempted to capture the most representative cases that you will have to remember, at least in the beginning of your report preparation. Each of the seven cases will be described in the following four parts:

- **Part 1:** *Find Pattern.* In this part, you will be given information that is typically found in items themselves; for example, if you have a book, you will find data elements including the name of the author, title, edition statement, publication place, publisher's name, and publication date. Together, these data elements, referred to as bibliographic information, are essential in bibliographic citing. Data elements may be scattered on both sides of the title page and not necessarily in that order. Now that you know which typical data elements make up a bibliographic citation, your goal is to find various bibliographic patterns.

- **Part 2:** *Give Answers.* You will be asked to answer a set of questions related to the information that is given in the source.

- **Part 3:** *Find Rules.* With a bibliographic style manual in hand (Turabian, 2007), you will need to find rules that correspond to your answers in Part 2. Start with the contents and the index in the *Manual.* You may need to use several chapters and several rules to answer the questions posed in Part 2 in order to cite a source.

- **Part 4:** *Apply Rules to Patterns and Cite.* Finally, you will provide a citation as the "answer." You may find that some patterns do not easily match rules. In these cases, apply the closest rules. More importantly, think of the main purposes of citing, as discussed earlier.

Case 1—Question #1: How to cite a book

- **Part 1:** As shown in Figure 9.1, a title page of the book you want to cite has the following information:

Thomas Hutchinson and the origins of the American Revolution	Additional information is given on the back of the title page:
Andrew S. Walmsley	Copyright ©1999 in the United States of America
New York University Press	
New York	

Figure 9.1: Title page of the book

- **Part 2:** To cite the above book, you need to answer the following questions:
    - How many authors are listed on the title page of this book?
    - What is the title of the book?
    - What about publication data?
        - (a) publication place:
        - (b) publisher's name:
        - (c) date of publication:

- **Part 3:** As mentioned earlier, for the purposes of this exercise, we will use Turabian's *Manual* (2007). We will use the reference list (RL) style (the Author-Date system), rather than bibliography (B) style (the Author-Title system).

- **Part 4:** If you are using the *Manual*, apply rules in order to cite the book. If you are not using the *Manual*, follow the template below in order to cite your own books that are written by a single author:

Template:

> Author's Last Name, First Name (Middle Name Initial, if given). Publication date. *Title of the book*. Publication Place: Publisher's Name.

Your answer:

> Walmsley, Andrew S. 1999. *Thomas Hutchinson and the origins of the American Revolution*. New York: New York University Press.

Figure 9.2: Bibliographic citation—books by a single author

Case 2—Question #2: How to cite an encyclopedia article (printed version)

Template:

> *Title of the Encyclopedia,* edition., s.v. (means that you looked under word) "name of the person or place or topic that you looked under."

Your answer:

> *World Book Encyclopedia,* 15th ed., s.v. "Hutchinson, Thomas."

Case 3—Question #3: How to cite an encyclopedia article (Web version)

Template:

> "Title of the article," *Title of the Encyclopedia online;* accessed <date that you looked up>; available from <URL address>

Your answer:

> "Adams Family," *Encyclopedia Britannica online;* accessed <July 17, 2007>; available from <http://school.eb.com>

Case 4—Question #4: How to cite a story in a collected work

- **Part 1:** In this example (see Figure 9.3), you will cite an individual story, which is part of a collected work. "Europe" by Henry James is one of 57 stories in *American Short Stories*. The title page has the following information:

> American Short Stories
>
> > Fifth Edition
>
> Eugene Current-Garcia and Bert Hitchcock, both from Auburn University
> ©1990 HarperCollins Publishers

Figure 9.3: Title page from an anthology of short stories

- **Part 2:** Again, we need to answer several questions:

> (a) Who selected these 57 stories?
> (b) Is the publication place given?
> (c) When was the 5th edition published?

- **Part 3:** Use rule 8.116 (for short poems).
For question b, use rule 8.52 (for place of publication); in particular, see rule 8.55 for cases where place of publication is not given; the abbreviation *n. p.* (for *no place*) is sufficient.

- **Part 4:** Follow the rules from the *Manual*, or use the template below to create your own bibliographic entries:

Template:

> Author's Last Name, First Name (Middle Name Initial, if given). Publication date of the entire book. "Title of the part you used." In *Title of the entire book*, ed. First Name, Last Name of the editor(s) who edited the entire book, pages. Place of publication : Publisher's Name.

Your answer:

> Hughes, Langston. 2000. "Minstrel man." In *Americans' favorite poems : The favorite poem project anthology*, ed. Robert Pinsky and Maggie Dietz, 131. New York : W. W. Norton.

Figure 9.4: Citation—collected works

Case 5—Question #5: How to cite an article

- **Part 1:** In your paper you might have borrowed some ideas from an article published in the *Atlantic Monthly* August 1999, vol. 284, 19 through 21. The author and title are as follows:

> Can coffee drinkers save the rain forest? by Jennifer Bingham Hull

Figure 9.5: Bibliographic data from a journal article

- **Part 2:** As we did in the previous two examples, we need to answer some questions before we can cite the above article. Answers to the following questions will determine which rules you will use.

  - What is the type of publication? Circle one only:

    book   newspaper article   magazine article

- How many authors have contributed to this writing?
- Where does the writing appear?
- Note all other data (publication year, volume number, pagination):

- **Part 3:** If you are using the *Manual*, try to find the most appropriate rules. One of the most important decisions is to establish that the paper is an **article in a journal**, which leads you to rule 11.39. Note that different rules apply to magazine and newspaper articles.

- **Part 4:** Here is a template that you can use to cite journal articles:

> Last Name, First Name (Middle Initial, if given). Publication date. Title of the article. *Title of the Magazine* volume number (Month issued): pages of your article.

If you replace the above data elements, the answer will be as follows:

> Bingham Hull, Jennifer. 1999. Can coffee drinkers save the rain forest. *Atlantic Monthly* 284 (August): 19-21.

Figure 9.6: Citation—journal article

Case 6—Footnotes, endnotes

Some of your teachers may recommend the use of footnotes or endnotes. A rule of thumb for footnotes and endnotes is as follows: each time you cite a publication in your paper you should do the following two things:

1. In your paper: Identify your cited reference with a raised Arabic numeral half a space above the line. Example:

   In a recent article on the air we inhale, we read that "although Los Angeles has the most polluted skies in the nation, it is one of the few cities where air quality has improved in recent decades."[1]

2. Cite the source either at the foot of the page (FOOTNOTE) below a short line, or at the end of the paper (ENDNOTE). Example for the footnote:

---

[1]James M. Lents and William J. Kelly, Cleaning the air in Los Angeles, *Scientific American* 269 (1993): 32-39.

Case 7—Cybercitation templates

General guidance for citing material on the Internet is outlined in the following template:

> Author's Last Name, First Name. "Title of Work," accessed <date>; available from <URL address>.

If you replace the above parts with the corresponding data from a Web page, your citations are as follows:

> Hoemann, George H. "The American Civil War," accessed <July 11, 2007>; available from <http://sunsite.utk.edu/civil-war>.

Figure 9.7: Citation—Web page

How to write summaries?

This last part of the chapter shows you how to summarize sources that you used in your research. To summarize means to briefly state key points of an item that you used in your own reports. In order to avoid plagiarism, and teachers are good at recognizing this, it is important for you to know how to **critically** summarize the book or any other material using your own words. The phrase "critically summarize" means that you will summarize a resource beyond restating its table of contents, connecting it to your writing and, perhaps, how useful it has been to your current project. See Appendix N which contains reproducible templates on summaries.

Tips:

1. An easy way to go about doing this is to divide the work into various sections relating to special features of the work, its organization, and so on.
2. You may first summarize a given work informally without using full sentences.
3. You can color code different parts of the text by importance, amount of information, and order you intend to use in your report.
4. Another technique is to graphically make clusters with similar information grouped in each separate cluster. For example, one cluster might include everything that is said about a character; a separate cluster could contain his or her relations with other people and events; another about his or her contributions to political ideas, and so forth.
5. An important part of writing a summary is understanding each word that you use in your own writing; having a dictionary or your textbook beside you might help you summarize efficiently and accurately. Note: *Encyclopedia Britannica*

on the Web <eb.school.com> contains an integrated *Webster's Dictionary,* which gives you the meaning of any word you double click on.

6. Asking questions will make your report stronger, more interesting, and insightful.

We present two examples: how to summarize a book, and another example for an article. Each source is first cited; then we introduce headings as temporary scaffolding to remind you of important points to consider in summarizing and reviewing your sources.

NOTE: There are five basic rules to remember whenever you summarize documents that you used in your reports:

- Use your own words and not the authors' words.

- Mention highlights only rather than everything that is discussed in the document you are annotating. Separate important things from less important ones; be selective. Remember that your summary will review and capture only the main points of the source you are citing expressing these points.

- Be critical of others' writings in a positive way. (Skepticism helps even when reviewing published materials).

- Include your own insight and understanding.

- Make connections. For example, how is the original source useful for your current project?

How to critically summarize a book: an example

U. S. Department of Health and Human Services. 2000. *Healthy People 2010: Understanding and Improving Health.* 2nd ed. Washington, DC: Government Printing Office; accessed <Oct. 10, 2007>; available from <www.healthypeople.gov>.

Summary: With clearly defined objectives (i.e., to increase quality and years of healthy life, and to eliminate health disparities), the report takes the position that the individual is almost inseparable from the health of the larger community and the nation. The report addresses emerging public health indicators. Special **features** include an extensive bibliography that follows the organization of the report. Appendix is subdivided into 28 leading health issues, presented alphabetically, from access to quality health services, chronic diseases, cancer, diabetes, and environmental quality, to immunization, mental disorders, obesity, respiratory diseases, STDs, and substance abuse. All are easily readable and understandable. In regard to **bias**, the publication provides current status of health and compares leading indicators from around the world. It does not cover opposing viewpoints on controversial issues. The information is well **organized**.

Accuracy/currency: Data are based on information compiled by the National Center for Health Statistics, Centers for Disease Control and Prevention. The report is also available on the Web free of charge <www.health.gov/healthypeople/> and maintained current. The information is intended for anyone interested in the most important public health issues.

How to critically summarize an article: an example

Raymer, Steve. "St. Petersburg, Capital of the Tsars." *National Geographic*. 184.6 (1993): 96-121.

Summary: Monument to the worldly aspirations of its namesake rule and his imperial successors, St. Petersburg (also known as Petrograd, or City of Peter, as well as Leningrad) has survived the communist years to rival Moscow as Russia's cultural center. The article also shows historical and city maps. In terms of **organization**, the article is typical of other magazine stories. It traces the city's rich and turbulent history since its birth in 1703, Russia's triumph over Napoleon in 1812, and the 1917 revolution. Special **features** are photographs of lavish mosaics gracing the Church of the Resurrection, ornate facades and opulent interiors of palaces, museums, theaters, and parks. The author uses a popular style of writing, with pictures of gleaming ballrooms, libraries, and gardens of the tsars of Russia. Steve Raymer, who is the author of the book *St. Petersburg,* is both writer and photographer.

What you have learned

This chapter covers the material that oftentimes instructors find peripherally valuable, self-explanatory, and easy to learn. The result is that most students do not know how to cite the work they use in their reports; do not give credit to ideas they use; do not appreciate the value of evidence that they need to consider in their writings and presentations; and, above all, do not know how to evaluate a given work.

This chapter is by no means comprehensive and exhaustive. However, it is important that you start understanding the power of citing and critical reading of information sources. This chapter has introduced you to the following terms and concepts. We gloss over only the most important terminology:

Archival sources
Information contained in personal papers, diaries, photo albums, and logs; manuscripts, drawings, and sketches; first editions, cultural artifacts, and other unique objects. Archival sources are acquired, preserved, described, and organized in archives, historical societies, museums, and libraries. They may be found at homes, educational, and other cultural institutions.

Bibliographic citation	A record in precise and consistent form that gives details about an item used in your work regardless of its format and medium; the item is typically identified and described with the following data elements: author's name, title, and publication information.
Bibliographic style manual	A document that offers guidance to writers on how to consistently cite works that are used in their writings. There are many different styles of citing printed and online sources.
Data elements	Unitary pieces of information that make up a bibliographic record. Examples include author's name, title, source where that item is published, and date of publication.
Formal communication	Recorded pieces of knowledge that are peer-reviewed (critically reviewed by a panel of experts on the accounts of content and style) and published in books, periodical literature, and audiovisual works.
Informal communication	Information that is transmitted through informal channels such as phone, fax, face-to-face dialogue, e-mail, blogs, wikis, and instant messaging.
Primary sources	Documents and art objects that contain novel ideas in humanities, social sciences, and sciences/engineering, new methods, and applications. Examples are: fiction writings, patents, period films, sound recordings, photographs, and prints.
Secondary sources	Secondary sources are published accounts that draw on primary sources; examples are textbooks, anthologies, and compilations of published writings. Reference sources such as encyclopedia articles are designed, through their structure, to rapidly give you needed information or reference to primary and secondary sources.
Summary (also known as annotation)	A summary, often called an abstract or annotation tells us what the document says. Depending on the nature of the document, content and format of the original writing, annotations may vary.

Think Guide   6

Honor Principle Discussed And Applied

Studies have demonstrated that those educational institutions with an Honor Principle have fewer incidents of plagiarism-related issues than institutions without such a document (reviewed in Ercegovac and Richardson, 2004). Furthermore, if the principle is discussed and applied consistently in curricular, classroom, and behavioral situations throughout the institution, it is even more powerful and useful than if it is merely mentioned as a concept and published in student handbooks and other documents.

Think Guide #6 uses Marlborough School Honor Principle. This author has assigned the Honor Principle to all incoming students; students select a particular characteristic from the Honor Principle (see keywords below in bold, emphasis by the author). In small groups of about three persons per group, students write brief essays highlighting selected ethical values (e.g., pride, respect, expectation, trust, commitment, responsibility, honesty, fairness). They relate each of these characteristics to their own personal relationships and experiences with their friends, parents, and teachers in different situations. Students share their experiences in a variety of ways with the class. Some like to highlight their reports on an accompanying two or three page PowerPoint presentation; others read their reports, and yet other groups perform their experiences in their own small working groups.

Each group looks up a dictionary definition for a selected characteristic as a starting point that they include in their reports.

The Honor Principle

We believe that to be **honorable** we must have honor and **pride** within ourselves and **trust** throughout our *school community*. Each student must **respect** not only herself but the *rights* and *property* of others. For the Honor Principle to work we all have to be willing to uphold these values. In order to operate within an Honor Principle a common understanding of these **expectations** must exist between faculty, administration, and students.

(Marlborough School, Los Angeles, California 2007, with permission to include in this book.)

Bibliography

Introduction

This author selected a body of literature that relates to various aspects of information literacy. Teachers and librarians who are already offering IL skills to their high school students will find many well-known writers and IL models throughout this bibliography. Others, who are thinking about designing their own programs, may find this bibliography useful as a survey of contributors from many different disciplines: librarians and educators, psychologists, and other researchers.

Mainly, we have searched the ProQuest Platinum database and other databases including ERIC database, Library & Information Science Abstracts, Psychological Abstracts, and Information Science Abstracts. We have also used other reports and the extensive personal files on this topic. This selected bibliography is organized under the following five headings:

- Standards: A common ground for learning.
- Information literacy models.
- Inquiry, assessment, ethical use of information.
- Information seeking: students' use of the Internet resources.
- Critical thinking.

1. Standards: A common ground for learning

American Association of School Librarians and Association for Educational Communications and Technology. *Information Power: Building Partnership for Learning.* Chicago: American Library Association, 1998.

American Association of School Librarians. *Standards for the 21st-Century Learner.* Chicago: American Library Association, 2007.

The new set of standards for school library media (SLM) programs emphasize the use of 21st century information skills, resources, and tools to:

- Inquire, think critically, and gain knowledge
- Draw conclusions, make informed decisions, apply knowledge to new situations, and create new knowledge
- Share knowledge and understanding with others and participate ethically and productively as members of our democratic society
- Pursue personal and aesthetic growth

Glancing over our preface in this book, these four sets of proposed learning skills (AASL, 2007) are fully compatible with the components of the learning theory that have been a part of both editions of this work. The components are content understanding, problem solving, self-reflection, collaboration, and communication.

Association of College & Research Libraries. *Standards for libraries in higher education.* Chicago: American Library Association, 2006. 10 Oct. 2006. <www.ala.org/ala/acrl/acrlstandards/standardslibraries.htm>.

The Boyer Commission on Educating Undergraduates, *Reinventing undergraduate education: A blueprint for America's research universities.* 1998. 13 Aug. 2006. <//naples.cc.sunysb.edu/Pres/boyer.nsf>.

DeBell, Matthew and Chris Chapman. "Computer and Internet use by students in 2003. Statistical analysis report." National Center for Education Statistics. Sept. 2006. Institute of Education Sciences. 21 Oct. 2007. <nces.ed.gov/pubsearch/pubsinfo.asp?pubid=2006065>.

Ercegovac, Zorana. "Bridging the knowledge gap between secondary and higher education," *College & Research Libraries.* 64.1 (2003a):75-85.

Ercegovac, Zorana. (2003b). "Bringing the library into the lab: How information literacy skills make better science students" *School Library Journal.* 49.2 (2003b):52-53.

Ercegovac, Zorana. Computer Science and Telecommunication Board (CSTB) and National Research Council. "Being fluent with information technology." National Academies Press, 1999.

International Society for Technology in Education (ISTE). *National educational technology standards for teachers.* Eugene, OR: ISTE, NETS Project, 2002. 21 Oct. 2007 <//cnets.iste.org/teachers>.

"National educational technology standards for students: The next generation." 22 Oct. 2007 <http://cnets.iste.org/students/pdf/NETS_for_Students_2007.pdf>.

National science education standards. 2001. Washington, DC.: National Academy Press. 21 Oct. 2007 <www.nap.edu/readingroom/books/nses/>.

Williams, Kate. (Spring 2003). "Literacy and computer literacy: Analyzing the NRC's Being Fluent with Information Technology." The Journal of Literacy and Technology, 3(1). 21 Oct. 2007; <www.literacyandtechnology.org/v3n1/williams.htm>.

2. Information literacy models

Classical information retrieval systems (IRS) were predominantly computer-centered and based on the premise that the searcher's information need represented in the form of a precise query would match a document represented in the form of document surrogates, producing the end result. Furthermore, IR systems in the pre-digital era were designed with little or no sensitivity toward the user. As demonstrated in the reported studies below, there is a room for the design of better IR systems that are usable by ordinary people, including children. One way to design user-centered IRs, especially in the digital context, is to look at how people, especially children, seek and search for information. We rarely see children searching in five or six or 10 or any fixed number of clear-cut steps in order to get information they need. Search experience is a more random process in which people accomplish their goal through a series of exploratory and iterative moves (Bates, 1989). Children constantly shift their focus as their knowledge evolves; they prefer pictorial and multimedia rich contents rather than print and bibliographic sources. They also incorporate feelings into their search process. Some of these information seeking models have been reported in selected studies below. Not only is it fascinating to learn about information seeking among children at different stages of their cognitive and physical development, but this knowledge can serve as a framework to designing richer and more sensitive IRs than it has been possible so far.

Bates, Marcia J. "The design of browsing and berrypicking techniques for the online search interface." Online Review. 13.5 (Oct. 1989): 407-424.

Eisenberg, Michael B. and Robert E. Berkowitz. "The six habits of highly effective students." School Library Journal. 41.8 (1995): 22-25.

Ercegovac, Zorana. Information literacy: Search strategies, tools & resources for high school students. Worthington, OH: Linworth Publishing, 2001.

Ercegovac, Zorana. "The interpretation of library use in the age of digital libraries: Virtualizing the name." Library & Information Science Research. 19.1 (1997): 31-46.

Kuhlthau, Carol C. "Accommodating the user's information search process: Challenges for information retrieval system designers." Bulletin of the American Society for Information Science. 25.3 (Feb/Mar 1999a): 12-16.

Kuhlthau, Carol C. "Learning in digital libraries: An information search process." Library Trends. 45 (1997): 708-724.

Kuhlthau, Carol C. "The role of experience in the information search process of an early career information worker: Perceptions of uncertainty, complexity, construction, and sources." Journal of the American Society for Information Science. 50.5 (1999b): 399-412.

Kuhlthau, Carol C. Seeking meaning: A process approach to library and information services 2nd ed. Westport, CT: Libraries Unlimited, 2004.

Leide, John E., Charles Cole, Jamshid Beheshti, Andrew Large, and Yang Lin. "Task-based information retrieval: Structuring undergraduate history essays for better course evaluation using essay-type visualization." Journal of the American Society for Information Science and Technology. 58.9 (2007):1,227-1,241.

Manduca, Cathryn A. and David W. Mogk. *Using data in undergraduate science classrooms. Final report on an interdisciplinary workshop held at Carleton College, April 2002.* Sponsored by the National Science Digital Library with funding from the National Science Foundation, Division of Undergraduate Education (Grant NSF-0127298). 2002.

Pitts, Judy M. "Mental models of information: The 1993-94 AASL/Highsmith Research Award study." School Library Media Quarterly. 23.3 (Spring 1995): 177-184.

The Science Teacher: Designing Inquiry Pathways, January 2004, 71(1). The entire issue is devoted to different aspects of scientific inquiry in teaching and learning science. See William Harwood, "An activity model for scientific inquiry: A new inquiry model offers a successful guide to how science is really done," pp. 44-46.

Stripling, Barbara K. "Learning-centered libraries: Implications from research." School Library Media Quarterly. 23.3 (Spring 1995): 163-170.

Vakkari, Pertti, and Kalervo Jarvelin. "Explanation in information seeking and retrieval." In Amanda Spink and C. Cole (eds.). New directions in cognitive information retrieval. Dordrecht, Netherlands: Springer, 2005: 113-138.

3. Inquiry, assessment, ethical use of information

Bertland, Linda H. "An overview of research in metacognition: Implications for information skills instruction." School Library Media Quarterly. Winter 1996: 96-99.

Chung, Gregory K. W. K., Herl, Howard E., Davina, C. D. Klein, O'Neil, Harold F., Jr., & John Schacter. Estimate of the potential costs and effectiveness of scaling up CRESST assessment software. CSE Technical Report 462. Center for the Study of Evaluation, *National Center for Research on Evaluation, Standards, and Student Testing*. Graduate School of Education & Information Studies at the University of California Los Angeles, Los Angeles, Dec. 1997.

For the CRESST cognitive model of learning, the reader is referred to a series of reports and excellent bibliographies by Eva L. Baker and her colleagues at the *Center for the Study of Evaluation, National Center for Research on Evaluation, Standards, and Student Testing* (CRESST). Graduate School of Education & Information Studies at the University of California Los Angeles, Los Angeles.

Doyle, Christina S. Outcome measures for information literacy within the National Education Goals of 1990. Final Report to National Forum on Information Literacy. Summary of Findings. (ED 351 033). 24 June 1992.

Harada, Violet H. and Joan M. Yoshina. Assessing learning: Librarians and teachers as partners. Westport, CT: Libraries Unlimited, 2005.

O'Neil, Harold F., Jr. and Jamal Abedi. Reliability and validity of a state metacognitive inventory: Potential for alternative assessment. Center for Student Evaluation (CSE) Technical Report 469. Los Angeles: CRESST. Excellent bibliography. The report is published as a journal article in 1996 in *Journal of Educational Research*, 89 (1996): 234-245.

Under the heading, from inquiry to assessment, ethical use of information along with students' perceptions of plagiarism, especially in the digital age, are critical; the selected list of entries on the topic is suggested below:

Dames, Matthew. "Understanding plagiarism and how it differs from copyright infringement." Computers in Libraries. 27.6 (2007):25-27. The entire June issue of *Computers in Libraries* is devoted to different aspects of information use.

Ercegovac, Zorana and John V. Richardson, Jr. "Academic dishonesty, plagiarism included, in the digital age: A literature review." College & Research Libraries. 65.4 (2004): 311-18.

Ercegovac, Zorana. "What students say they know, feel, and do about cyber-plagiarism and academic dishonesty? A case study." In Proceedings of the American Society for Information Science and Technology (ASIST) "Sparking synergies: Bringing research and practice together." Charlotte, North Carolina, 28 Oct.-2 Nov. 2005. <www.asis.org/Conference/AM05/abstracts/42.html>.

"New frontiers in cheating." Encyclopædia Britannica. 2007. Encyclopædia Britannica Online School Edition. 20 July. <school.eb.com/eb/article-228894>.

Simpson, Carol. Copyright for schools: A practical guide. 4th ed. Columbus, OH: Linworth Publishing, 2005.

5. Information seeking: students' use of the Internet resources

The fourth group of studies has looked at information seeking behavior of students in high schools and colleges, as they interact with electronic sources, especially the Internet. With several exceptions, each study contains an extensive selection of studies in their respective bibliographies.

Ackerman, Elise. "Podcasting: it's not just for geeky types anymore." Seattle Times, 27 Nov. 2006: C3. This author reminds us that about one in eight baby boomers has downloaded a podcast.

Agosto, E. Denise. "A model of young people's decision-making in using the Web." Library and Information Science Research. 24 (2002): 311-341. The investigator studied high school girls and their coping mechanisms in searching Web-based contents.

Agosto, E. Denise and Sandra Hughes-Hassell. "Toward a model of the everyday life information needs of urban teenagers, part 1: Theoretical model." Journal of American Society for Information Science and Technology. 57.10 (2006): 1394-1403.

Agosto, E. Denise and Sandra Hughes-Hassell. "Toward a model of the everyday life information needs of urban teenagers, part 2: Empirical model." Journal of American Society for Information Science and Technology. 57.11 (2006): 1418-1426.

Baumann, Michael. Pew Internet releases report on Web 2.0. Information Today. 24.1 (Jan. 2007):13. While e-mail is still the most common Internet activity, online photo sharing is on the rise with 34 percent of Internet users surveyed in this study.

Bilal, Dania. "Children's use of the Yahooligans! Web search engine: I. Cognitive, physical, and affective behaviors on fact-based search tasks." Journal of American Society for Information Science and Technology. 51.7 (2000): 646-665.

Bleakey, A., Merzel, C.R., VanDevanter, N.L., and P. Messeri. "Computer access and Internet use among urban youth." American Journal of Public Health, 94.5 (2004): 744-746.

Chelton, Mary K. and Colleen Cool, eds. Youth information-seeking behavior: Theories, models, and issues. 2nd ed. Lanham, MD: Scarecrow Press, 2007.

Chung, Jin Soo and Delia Neuman. "High school students' information seeking and use for class projects." Journal of the American Society for Information Science and Technology, 58.10 (2007): 1503-1517.

Dresang, Eliza T. "The information-seeking behavior on youth in the digital environment." Library Trends. 54.2 (Fall 2005): 178-196.

Edwards, S. and B. Poston-Anderson. "Information, future time perspectives, and young adolescent girls: Concerns about education and jobs." Library & Information Science Research. 18 (1996): 207-223.

Ercegovac, Zorana. 2008. "Is the Google generation information literate? A case study with secondary school students." In *Proceedings of the Annual Meeting of the American Society for Information Science and Technology*, Columbus, OH. Paper accepted for presentation.

Fidel, Raya, et al. "A visit to the information mall: Web searching behavior of high school students." Journal of the American Society for Information Science. 50.1 (1999): 24-37.

Griffiths, J.R. and P. Brophy. "Student searching behavior and the Web: Use of academic resources and Google." Library Trends. 53.4 (2005): 539-554.

Hughes-Hassell, S. and E. T. Miller. "Current trends in public library Web sites for young adults: Meeting the needs of today's teens online." Library & Information Science Research. 25 (2003):1-14.

Kalbach, James. "'I'm feeling lucky': The role of emotions in seeking information on the Web." 2003. 1 Oct. 2007. <home.earthlink.net/~searchworkshop/docs/JKalbach_Emotions-InformationSeeking-Web_short21.pdf >.

Kupperman, J. and B.J. Fishman. "Academic, social, and personal uses of the Internet: Cases of students from an urban Latino classroom." Journal of Research on Technology in Education. 34 (2002): 189-215.

Large, A. "Children, teenagers, and the Web." ed. B. Cronin. Annual Review of Information Science and Technology, Medford, NJ: Information Today, 39 (2005): 347-392.

Latrobe, K. and W.M. Havener. "Information-seeking behavior of high school honor students: An exploratory study." Journal of Youth Services in Libraries. 10 (1997): 188-200.

Levin, D., Arafeh, S., Lenhart, A., and L. Rainie. "The digital disconnect: The widening gap between internet-savvy students and their schools." Pew Internet and American Life Project, 2002.

Online Computer Library Center (OCLC). "Perceptions of libraries and information resources," 2005. 9 July 2007. <www.oclc.org/reports/2005perceptions.htm>.

Savolainen, R. and Kari, J. "Placing the Internet in information source horizons: A study of information-seeking by Internet users in the context of self-development." Library & Information Science Research. 26 (2004): 415-433.

Shenton, A. K. and P. Dixon. "Issues arising from youngsters' information seeking behavior." Library and Information Science Research. 26.3 (2004): 177-200.

Todd, R.J. "Adolescents of the information age: Patterns of information seeking and use, and implications for information professionals." School Libraries Worldwide. 9.2 (2003): 27-46.

6. Critical thinking

Beyer, Barry K. "Critical thinking: What is it?" Social Education, 49.4 (April 1985): 270-76.

Doherty, John J. "Teaching information skills in the information age: the need for critical thinking." Library Philosophy and Practice. 1.2 (1999): 1-10.

Drueke, Jeanetta. "Active learning in the university library instruction classroom." Research Strategies. 10.2 (Spring 1992): 77-83.

Keller, J.M. "The systematic process of motivational design." Performance and Instruction. (Nov/Dec 1987): 1-8.

Payne, G. Phillip. "Environmental education and curriculum theory." Journal of Environmental Education. 35.1 (2006): 1-12.

Small, Ruth V. "An exploration of motivational strategies used by library media specialists during library and information skills instruction." School Library Media Quarterly. 2 (1999): 1-22.

Twigg, Carol A. "Improving learning and reducing costs: New models for online learning." Educause Review. (Sept/Oct 2003): 28-38.

Waldman, Micaela. "Freshmen's use of library electronic resources and self-efficacy." Information Research. 8.2 (Jan. 2003): 1-32.

Weiler, Angela. "Information-seeking behavior in generation Y students: Motivation, critical thinking, and learning theory." Journal of Academic Librarianship. 31.1 (2005): 46-53.

Wesley, Theresa. "Teaching library research: Are we preparing students for effective information use?" Emergency Librarian. 18.3 (Jan/Feb 1991): 23-24, 26-30.

Appendix A (especially for educators)
Alignment Between Technology and IL Standards

Because this text may be used by a wide range of educators, we first want to remind our readers of the Information Literacy (IL) standards for secondary schools (Table A1); then, six broad categories of Information Technology (IT) standards (ISTE's NETS) are presented in Table A2. A crossover among IL standards is described in Table A3.

According to the national K-12 school library standards (AASL, 2007) learners use skills, resources, and tools to:

1. Inquire, think critically, and gain knowledge.
2. Draw conclusions, make informed decisions, apply knowledge to new situations, and create new knowledge.
3. Share knowledge and participate ethically and productively as members of our democratic society.
4. Pursue personal and aesthetic growth.

Table A1: *Standards for the 21st-Century Learner* (AASL, 2007)

National Educational Technology Standards for All Students: The Next Generation was developed by the International Society for Technology in Education. ISTE has revised the standards for secondary students as follows:

1. Creativity and innovation underline creative thinking and develop products and processes using technology (e.g., use models and simulations to explore complex systems and issues).
2. Communication and collaboration activities use digital media to communicate and work collaboratively.
3. Research and information fluency encourage the use of digital tools to gather, evaluate, and use information.
4. Critical thinking, problem-solving, and decision-making are used to plan and conduct research, manage projects, solve problems, and make informed decisions using appropriate digital tools and resources.
5. Digital citizenship relates to understanding human, cultural, and societal issues related to technology as well as to ethical behavior.
6. Technology operations and concepts relates to students' selection and use of technologies, and troubleshooting systems and applications.

Table A2: ISTE's NETS(S)

Table A3 presents a crossover between IL *Standards for the 21st-Century Learner* and ISTE's NETS-S.

Standards for the 21st-Century Learner (AASL, 2007) along skills, dispositions, responsibilities, and self-assessment strategies	NETS-S (ISTE, 2007)
1. Inquire, think critically, and gain knowledge (use prior knowledge as context for learning; find, evaluate, and select resources, master technologies, and use ethically).	4. Critical thinking, problem solving to manage projects and make informed decisions using appropriate resources. 3. Use of digital resources to gather, evaluate, and use information.
2. Draw conclusions, make informed decisions, apply knowledge to new situations, and create new knowledge, e.g., inquiry-based process; organize information, collaborate.	1. Creativity and innovation in thinking and product development. 2. Communication and collaboration activities use digital media to communicate and work collaboratively.
3. Share knowledge and participate ethically and productively as members of our democratic society.	5. Digital citizenship: understanding cultural and societal issues related to technology and ethical behavior.
4. Pursue personal and aesthetic growth.	

Table A3: Crossover of standards: IL 7-12, IL-HE, NETS

Appendix B (especially for educators)
Goals and Means to Achieve Them

Unique features of this 2nd edition, *Information Literacy: Search Strategies, Tools & Resources for High School Students and College Freshmen*, are described and organized under the following three goals.

GOAL #1: Bridging Multiple Literacies. Information technologies have become ubiquitous and used at homes, schools, libraries, labs, cybercafés, airports, and workplaces. A study from the National Center for Education Statistics (NCES) reports that in Fall 2003, nearly 100 percent of U.S. public schools had some form of Internet access, compared with 35 percent in 1994. People use IT everywhere in various contexts to achieve specific goals. Therefore, this edition integrates Information Literacy (IL) and technology skills within collaborative projects. Students will, for example, learn to use the acquired skills to look up topics in electronic databases and search engines, to understand how heterogeneous information and data sets are organized and digitally represented, to critically evaluate the retrieved information, and to ethically use information. All these skills are important in order for the learners to solve problems, draw conclusions, use evidence, create new knowledge, ask further questions, and pursue personal and aesthetic growth (*Standards for the 21st-Century Learner*, 2007).

Means to Achieve Goal #1

To integrate standards in IL, IT, and content standards under a single umbrella, we provide suggestions for educators to organize collaborative projects in the sciences (Appendix E), arts (Appendix F), and social sciences (Appendix G) that are aligned with the standards and appropriate for high school students and college freshmen.

High school projects have been compiled since 1998 and come from this author's daily collaboration with instructors and technology coordinators; ideas for college projects are drawn from close interaction with UCLA students since 1991, from other college instructors, and course descriptions nationwide. Each project, based on authentic inquiries, has been classroom tested and fine tuned. Given in appendices D-G, each sample project may be modified for specific preferences.

GOAL #2: Bridging the Gap between High School Students and College Freshmen via IL and Technology (IL&T) Standards. This edition focuses on one of the most significant transitions that students face, that from high schools to colleges. While students are only some 2-3 months apart from their high school graduation to entering colleges, information literacy, for example, is often treated separately, one set of standards concerned with 7-12th grade students (AASL, 2007); another for college students (AC&RL, 2000). In addition, today's high school students who enroll in Advanced Placement courses will find this text an invaluable resource.

Means to Achieve Goal #2

In order to bridge the gap between high schools and colleges, the two sets of standards are fused into a synthetic one, and whenever practical, showcased in sample classroom projects (Ercegovac, 2003a). Specific ways we can help students transition into college library environments will be demonstrated at each of the decision making points in the research process. Examples include:

1. College students are encouraged to be more responsible in their management of time, selection of resources, and research process; they are often asked to propose a topic for research projects. Typically, high school students are not given that initiative and are often presented with a menu of possible topics they could choose from.
   Our approach: Develop research honor seminar courses in which high school students gain independence in choosing and managing their research topics, projects, and process. This author gave UCLA college students the flexibility to select topics they were interested in; others researched topics for their concurrent classes; they wrote a bibliographic essay and focused on literature review rather than the topic itself. This is a challenge to many students as they tend to write about the topic rather than meta-analysis of literature on the chosen topic.

2. College and research libraries organize their collections following the Library of Congress Classification; high school students become comfortable with the Dewey Decimal Classification which is vastly different from LCC.
   Our approach: Both DDC and LCC are provided in Appendix H. The purpose of classification is reviewed and main properties may be applied in searching library catalogs. Compare the difference between DDC and LCC for Roosevelt's administration (973.911 in DDC vs. E 756-760 in LCC), for physics (530 in DDC vs. QC in LCC), or aerospace engineering (629.1 vs. TL).

3. College students are often required to compile their own bibliography of sources for their projects; high school students are often given a reading list for the projects.
   Our approach: Instructors should use less scaffolding in their lectures; students should be exploring the literature before committing themselves to something that is either too broad or too specific and technical.

4. College students are often asked to read on their own in order to discuss an issue in class; high school students often expect to have the material explained in class.

Our approach: Assign higher assessment weight on class participation based on assigned readings; ask students to bring questions and lead discussion on their topics.

GOAL #3: Layering Information. Another contribution of the 2008 edition is this

author's belief that we need to **focus on** *customized learning* and *research processes* that are *measurable* and *holistic.* While students, instructors, and other users of this text might have different information needs, all need to know a stock of IL skills, resources, and tools that would make them successful learners and researchers.

Means to Achieve Goal #3

In order to make information relevant to different audiences, this edition provides the main stock of skills for all readers. In addition, sections are designated especially relevant for students (Appendix C), and others of special interest to instructors (Appendices A-B).

In summary, information literacy has been traditionally influenced by *resource-intensive* approaches; since the *Information Power* publication (AASL & AECT), we have seen a relatively successful push beyond bibliographic instruction toward understanding authentic inquiry-based IL skills and information use (AASL; AC&RL). Technology coordinators have also shifted their focus from *technology-intensive* skills to questions such as, how do we incorporate technology tools into curriculum and learning (ISTE's NETS)?

As instructors have increasingly become technologically and IL savvy, we have seen yet a new wave, especially among younger instructors; instructors more aggressively than before integrating technologies and various resources in their lesson plans. The result is an undivided control of their classroom space and time, and less collaboration with librarians; this push has created a need for in-service capacity building support for instructors. So, while librarians might get less classroom contact with students, there may be more opportunity to teach the teachers, parents, administrators, and technology coordinators in the use of innovative ways to customize research moments for specific projects, needs, and individual or group preferences.

Therefore, in order to bridge gaps across technological literacy and information literacy, this edition will focus on *learning and research skills* that every high school graduate should have before entering his or her college freshman year; similarly, every college freshman who had been exposed to the material presented in this edition should be successful in achieving his or her academic and personal goals.

Table B1 on page 143 identifies areas that we need to pay special attention. Area A is mainly represented in IL standards rather than in NETS-S. We should continue to work on integrating IL concepts and skills into research experiences (Area B). All types of resources need to be used and not just digital resources. Area C, while mainly the instructors' territory, could be better shared with librarians. The least developed area deals with self-reflection, feedback, and cognition (Area D).

(A) Understand requirements and performance criteria, comfort level with skills (review materials, identify gaps); clarify, recognize information need, ask questions, get ready for library research phase: to seek, locate, retrieve, evaluate, and use. (B) This preparatory phase has been left mainly to **instructors**; typically, projects are defined by classroom teachers and assigned to students (from a pre-selected menu of topics); teachers often in a hurry coordinate projects with librarians and tech coordinators.	(B) Seek/evaluate/retrieve consists of well known IL steps that typically include activities of exploring via browsing, accessing (search terms, Boolean operators, limiting features, search syntax, and modification), finding, locating, evaluating, retrieving, and discarding unwanted items. Although "use" has also been included, needs more attention. Pursues personal growth, enjoys literature and other creative expressions of information, strives for knowledge generation. This phase has been traditionally covered by **librarians** (LMS) who have fully embraced *Standards for the 21st-Century Learner* (AASL, 2007).
(D) More attention is required in understanding the role of feedback, self reflection, revision, and perception of the task; in content understanding and in problem solving contexts, the pedagogical divide among LMS, instructors & technology coordinators, self reflection on group experiences, the teacher's perspective on "seeing students' thinking," reflection on how levels of explanation impact students' understanding. This area offers promise for opportunities and potential partnerships.	(C) The phase in which students begin to collect relevant material has been the most challenging for students; it is here that many higher order thinking processes are made, evidence is re-evaluated, analyzed, synthesized, cited and summarized, integrated, explained, and communicated in papers, scrapbooks, albums, films, plays, dance, music, or cartoons. This phase has been handled partially by librarians (bibliographies, annotations to a certain degree, and ethical use of information sources). Most of the cognitive processes have been traditionally dealt with by classroom teachers.

Table B1: Toward Learning and Research Literacy

Toward this goal, the National Education Technology Plan <http://www.ed.gov/about/offices/list/os/technology/plan/2004/site/edlite-default.html> published major action steps and recommendations; among other points, we need to strengthen leadership such as partnerships with higher education and community, and improve teacher education.

When asked about their use of technology, more than 55,000 respondents across all educational sectors in urban and rural schools wanted to see plenty of digital devices that are wearable, wireless, voice activated, with high speed connectivity to the Internet, with features such as CD/DVD player and burner, USB port, MP3 player, iPod, digital camera, cell phone, planner, instant messaging, access to electronic sources and study guides—a sort of digital Swiss army knife. They also want to learn and complete their assignments online with intelligent tutors especially in math and the sciences. Increasingly, we will witness proliferation of technology that will be used in searching, communicating, and learning. Special attention is required in the area of policy matters. Now that we have multiple technologies in place every-where anytime, we need to set boundaries on how to use these devices ethically and responsibly.

Secondary schools are ideally positioned to work with educators, technology coordinators, administrators, and researchers through partnerships with higher educa-tion, building 7-16th grade teachers' capacity, and the deployment of virtual learning. Sandwiched between middle school and college education, high school educators have a privileged place to design, pilot, and evaluate customized, sequenced learn-ing, and contextualized technologies especially in interdisciplinary inquiries.

Appendix C (especially for students)
College Libraries Are Not Just Larger School Libraries

Let's take a moment and remind ourselves of some of these differences that you will notice as you transition from high school to college libraries. These are time and effort saving tips that work, so pay close attention.

Transitioning to college-level research: Managing projects and feelings

We are listing some of the points that you will notice as you leave your familiar high school libraries and venture for research experiences in your college libraries.

- **Research topic selection: From low risk pre-selected topics by your teacher toward a higher responsibility (and higher risk) of your self-selected topics.** In secondary schools, teachers will typically assign project topics; alternatively, you may select a topic from a menu of pre-selected choices. In upper level high school grades and beginning undergraduate seminars, you will be increasingly given a responsibility to select your own topic. This may not be as easy as it initially appears to be. You will sharpen the topic's perspective by surveying the territory, by consulting with teachers and advisors as many times as necessary as you negotiate a special angle, time period or style, and locate the materials that will become your seed literature.

- **Project management skills.** A research project is normally presented by your teacher in the form of a well thought out document; typically, she will subdivide the project into subheadings such as introduction, objectives of the project, main parts, grading and performance rubrics, timeline for specific parts, detailed guidelines for written part, as well as for presentation, if required, with sample pages attached in back of the document. You will be required to provide evidence for your claims in the form of a bibliography for sources and ideas you used in your writings. As soon as you obtain the handout, or project description, you will read carefully all points and requirements and make sure that each fine detail is understood, and if necessary, clarified. A part of this skill is to open the word document for your initial table of contents, another file for note taking, and yet another for bibliographic citations that will eventually become a part of your paper.

- **You are required to ask good questions.** Many high school students and college freshmen might think that asking questions may look as if you are "lost" or "stupid." Nothing of that is true; in fact, it is your responsibility to ask the right people the right questions; that too is an acquired skill. This means that you understand that library instructors are experienced in dealing with these situations, that they expect you to visit them or make appointments to go over the best sources to use for your level of aptitude and requirements. In order to be efficient, you need to ask exactly what you need, and not to "make it easier" and make the topic broader or a bit different than it actually is.

- **It is all right to be nervous and excited.** It is perfectly fine to have mixed feelings about your project. During this initial phase, when you are assigned your topic, or you have volunteered a topic you are passionate about, you may appear both confused and enthusiastic. It may be confusing if you lack technical vocabulary skills, if the environment is new or too competitive, materials are inadequate, time is unrealistic, etc. One of the main shortcomings may be lack of understanding what you are asked to do, how to precisely do it, where to ask for help, and what to ask in order to clarify possible confusions. Some of you may feel eager to learn something new if you are motivated, if you welcome challenges, if you are open minded, and if you are ready to face opportunities.

- **Vocabulary builder: Where to harvest the words (a.k.a. keywords)?** You have probably noticed that many teachers will tell you to just enter some keywords into search engines and online databases (that too applies to searching printed sources such as encyclopedias); however, if you are a novice in the rather complex topic, you really DON'T have relevant words to search under. You will learn next where to find those "keywords" (see point #5 below).

Finally, you are in the college library, then what? Once you have clarified your topic's boundaries and expectations, you will be visiting your library as a class or on your own. In either situation, a recipe for effective research is to:

1. Familiarize yourself with the library layout, read signage, announcements, and turn off your cell phone.
2. Have your assignment in front of you (remember that your topic should drive your research, not the sources you will find in the library).
3. Get a laptop for note taking (or equivalent, such as reference cards) as well as a copy of the bibliographic style manual that your school prefers.
4. Obtain library primer that your teacher and/or librarian have designed specifically for this project or class of projects; there are similarities across all research projects and specifics for science versus art history projects.
5. Learn new vocabulary and understand how concepts are interrelated with one another; these will help you in looking up literature on the selected topic. Conceptual mapping may be helpful to draw on a paper showing broader and narrower topics, specific relationships between concepts and terms; these would be helpful in finding search words in looking up materials.
6. Familiarize yourself with basic classes of sources (in-house, through interlibrary loan, online databases) and access systems to locate books, journal articles, cartoons, films, posters and photos, music, and digital primary sources.

7. Demystify some of the widely held beliefs that the Web is like a giant encyclopedia written by experts, that anything on a Web is worth including in your research project, and that you don't have to cite sources that you used on the Web.

8. Know the best first sources for your topic (and if you don't, ask and learn how to use them efficiently—it is likely that you will use them again and often during high school and college).

9. Take notes, learn to summarize, and write bibliography.

10. Familiarize yourself with basic technology skills during this initial phase; you will soon be using various technologies such as graphing and statistical packages, presentation software, multimedia editing, and Web authoring tools.

11. Learn that the research process is spiral, iterative, cumulative, and contextualized; learn to modify your initial table of contents and update your bibliography (as some sources might be discarded and updated with more relevant ones).

Each of these points can be elaborated on, but these main points will get you started, reduce anxiety, and give you more time to spend on more interesting tasks.

Appendix D (especially for educators)
Getting Started with Primary Sources

Use of primary sources: Digging deep into History

By using the primary sources, you as educators will have the opportunity to discuss primary sources (also known as cultural heritage artifacts) as evidence, and, when appropriate, explain concepts such as "manuscripts," "records," "provenance," "original order," "intellectual property," and "fair use." In addition, each primary source should be discussed with regard to its creator(s), main purpose of an artifact, intended audience, date of creation (of text, cartoon, photograph, moving picture, interview, choreography, music), and its broader context.

Examples of primary sources

The following links include numerous digital primary sources for lesson plans and classroom exercises. The Library of Congress National Digital Library suggests activities for students to work with artifacts, manuscripts, photographs, posters, and music, that are compatible with curriculum standards and information literacy skills. "Using primary sources in the classroom," along with lesson plans organized by theme, topic, discipline, and era, are at:

<http://memory.loc.gov/ammem/ndlpedu/lessons/primary.html>

The Library's link also gives samples for source types such as:

a) Objects including period artifacts, tools, coins, weapons, uniforms, fashion, tombstones

b) Images such as photos, films, video, fine art

c) Audio such as oral histories and interviews, music, and sound recordings

d) Statistics such as census data, maps, ordinances, blueprints, and architectural drawings

e) Textual sources including cookbooks, advertisements, journals, letters, postcards, and diaries

f) Family photographs, papers, local historical societies, local buildings, and public places

g) Legal, financial, and health documents

h) Tickets (to concerts, museums, ski runs), announcements, museum catalogs, and television programs

i) Patents as primary sources for inventions and new technological advances

j) Raw scientific data such as satellite pictures of the moons and other planets

k) Newspaper stories from the historical periods, such as *New York Times* (going back to 1855). Also see the Library of Congress, The Making of America, The National Archives and Records Administration, and many others

l) Furniture pieces (do you watch "Antiques Roadshow" on PBS?)

Calisphere is the University of California's Digital Library free public gateway to a world of primary sources. More than 150,000 digitized items—including photographs, documents, newspaper pages, political cartoons, art pieces, diaries, transcribed oral histories, advertising, and other unique cultural artifacts reveal the diverse history and culture of California and its role in national and world history. Calisphere's content has been selected from the libraries and museums of the UC campuses, and other cultural heritage organizations: <www.calisphere.universityof-california.edu>.

Numerous images are organized under the following themes:

1848-1865:   Gold Rush Era
1870-1900:   Closing the Frontier
1900-1940s: Emerging Industrial Order
1929-1939:   The Great Depression
1939-1945:   World War II
1950s-1970s: Social Reform (e.g., the Civil Rights Movement; the Free Speech Movement; Watts; Struggle for Social Justice)

<www.calisphere.universityofcalifornia.edu/themed_collections/>

A variety of primary sources have been collected into sets that support the California Content Standards in History-Social Sciences, English-Language Arts, and Visual Arts for use in K-12 classrooms. These collections of primary sources make it easy for teachers to find the materials they need quickly:

■ Themed Collections <www.calisphere.universityofcalifornia.edu/themed_collec-tions/index.html>: Primary sources organized into historical eras with brief overviews that provide historical context.

■ California Cultures <www.calisphere.universityofcalifornia.edu/calcultures/>: Images of four ethnic groups—African-Americans, Asian Americans, Hispanics Americans, and Native Americans.

■ Japanese American Relocation Digital Archive <jarda.cdlib.org/>: Personal and official documents, transcribed oral histories, and works of art bring viewers inside the Japanese-American internment experience during World War II.

■ Browse A-Z <www.calisphere.universityofcalifornia.edu/browse-a-z.html>: This alphabetical list of terms selected from the California Content Standards makes it easy to locate primary sources for classroom use.

Examples for projects with primary sources

Ask students to take pictures of their favorite buildings, bridges, resorts, parks, museums and other cultural monuments; next, ask them to compare these with objects as represented on historical photographs. Ask them to describe each of the photos and assign labels so that their friends would be able to search and find them. One of my favorite places is Yosemite Valley in the Eastern Sierra Nevada in California. I often compare my own amateurish photos to those from the Yosemite Museum, and recently some amazing old photographs assembled in "Images of America Yosemite Valley" (Radanovich, 2004). Additional 19th century photos are here:
http://www.calisphere.universityofcalifornia.edu/themed_collections/subtopic1d.html

Other examples for projects with digital primary sources:

- Family Tree. Start with students' own families; have them make a family tree and include relatives that they personally know, that they heard about, and the places they have come from. How far back can they go? Which evidence would you use to investigate their professions, places, and family members? Ask them to interview some of the members.

- My School Stories. Examine your own school or college history. What questions would you bring? What evidence would you use to research your questions?

- Community Connections. There is history everywhere we go; so let's bring this wealth of information to our classrooms, motivate students to ask questions, research these questions, and report results back to the classroom. Now that we have our standards on the Web, we can see how important it is to blend labs and libraries together, how to prepare both written and oral presentations, and how important it is to learn to research individually and collaboratively. Technology is an important part of our management skills, accessing electronic resources, and using tools to put students' results in Web portfolios, podcasting and blogging programs, or digital videos.

- Classroom discussion may include issues that pertain to reformatting the same work into multiple formats; are digital and analog photographs the same? How about the social context of viewing or hearing an artifact or a piece of music? Are there ethical considerations in reformatting or rendering an artifact?

Behavioral change

The reviewed literature and our own experience suggest that students "google" first before using peer-reviewed reputable resources. This book suggests several excellent Web-based sources that may be used in addition to printed ones. Examples are digital libraries of primary sources and other documents (organized thematically, or by collections) that students can use across disciplines for a variety of projects and tasks. By using digital primary sources, students can get a feel for a variety of formats and notations that are represented digitally. They can compare digital sources with their printed equivalents on:

- Ease of use, navigation, desire to go back
- Effectiveness of finding information required for a particular task
- Precision of information retrieved
- Amount of information retrieved
- Presence of evidence

Again, as in the previous paragraph, this capacity to use high quality digital resources is at the heart of Information Literacy programs.

With the advent of wireless connectivity and plentiful computers, students tend to "cut and paste" portions of Web pages and implant those into their own projects (Ercegovac, 2005). Often borrowed ideas and paraphrased texts are not properly given credit; some students plagiarize intentionally or in ignorance. This author feels that it is the responsibility of educators to design programs for teachers, administrators, students, and parents in order to ensure that students use materials ethically and creatively.

Not all resources are equally well organized and valid. Table D1 shows some of the high quality digital sources that have become available to us through digitization efforts of the best collections in the United States. Digital libraries may be divided into those that group resources by topic or theme, thus we call them thematic digital libraries. Institutions like the Library of Congress, the Smithsonian Institution, and other museums, archives, and libraries digitize their physical collections and make them available virtually for classroom use and in projects like yours.

Digital Libraries	DL are systems that include collections and their descriptions (metadata), search, discovery, and retrieval functionalities, learning tools, community of users, digital rights management, and preservation and archival activities.
Thematic digital libraries, DL, are based around core disciplines or clusters of inter-related themes, such as DLESE (Digital Library for Earth System Education) <http://www.dlese.org> and NSDL (National Science DL) <http://nsdl.org>	**DLESE**—provides more efficient discovery of quality materials than search engines or library catalogs; Example: search and compare results on change over time on DLESE and GOOGLE; discuss! >provides safe Web-based environment; >includes lesson plans, expertise, lab activities, datasets (ex., real-time weather and water data, animation, virtual field trips, peer reviewed collections by educators and scientists; >standard-minded and focused on authentic inquiries). Examples: watershed game as a computer activity to help you manage your watershed: <www.bellmuseum.org/distancelearning/watershed/watershed2.html> By limiting a keyword to "dlese," one can harvest studies, reports, and other resources that would be hard to find without qualifying it to a specific DL (e.g., water quality dlese, global warming dlese, cloud formation dlese <http://ww2010.atmos.uiuc.edu/Gh)/home.rxml>.
Collection-based DL with in-house contents (Library of Congress, California DL, museums, archives, and historical societies). The Making of America project contains scanned sources from books, scholarly papers, and primary documents.	Digitized portions of collections make them remotely accessible to those populations who would not have otherwise had access to them. The American Memory <memory.loc.gov> includes primary sources as prints, posters, photographs, sound recordings, early films, images, maps, choreography, manuscripts, and other artifacts, along with lesson plans and technology tools. Other DLs are the Smithsonian National Museum of Natural History <www.mnh.si.edu>, Franklin Institute Science Museum <sln.fi.edu>, Exploratorium <www.exploratorium.edu>, Victoria and Albert Museum <www.vam.ac.uk> and historical societies (e.g., the New York Historical Society <www.AmRevOnline.org>. The Making of America <http://moa.umdl.umich.edu>.

Table D1: Examples of Digital Libraries

Appendix E (especially for educators)
Science Projects in Context

Introduction

Science content standards (National Science Education Standards <http://newton.nap.edu/html/nses> outline basic abilities and concepts for grades 7-12) across physical sciences (e.g., structure of atoms, structure and properties of matter, chemical reactions, motions and forces, conservation of energy and increase in disorder, interactions of energy and matter); life sciences (e.g., the cell, molecular basis of heredity, biological evolution, interdependence of organisms, matter, energy, and organization in living systems, behavior of organisms); and earth and space sciences (e.g., energy in the earth system, geochemical cycles, origin and evolution of the earth system, origin and evolution of the universe). Standards for science and technology (E), and science in personal and social perspectives (F) take into account various relationships between scientific and societal concerns, such as community health, population growth, natural resources, environmental quality, and natural and human-induced hazards (NSES, pp. 190-204).

The science standards offer useful frameworks in order to prepare students to address *authentic complex problems*, use *scientific methods*, *critically evaluate the validity of data or evidence*, and get the opportunity to *communicate results* verbally, in writing, or graphically. An example of interdisciplinary projects may be to study the impact of air and water quality in New York on certain populations; the variables may include different socioeconomic status (SES), age, race or ethnicity, gender, or disability. Another project may investigate impact of secondhand tobacco smoke on newborns.

Focusing on the *life science* content standards, projects may be designed to study an impact salt build-up has in Mojave Desert, California; impact of irrigation and erosion in the Everglades (freshwater) and what is done to alleviate this problem; influence of acid deposition in Canadian Boreal Forest, or how hydroelectric turbines affect the decline of salmon runs in the Columbia River Basin <http://www.efw.bpa.gov/publications/H08104-1.pdf>. Students might investigate levels of hazardous substances some professions may be exposed to in their routine work; excellent free-of-charge electronic sources include Haz-Map under TOXNET databases <http://toxnet.nlm.mih.gov> [HSDB, IRIS, CCRIS, GENE-TOX, ITER], and the Environmental Protection Agency's Toxic Release Inventory database, which gives toxic releases into water, air, and soil.

Ecology research projects will be especially relevant if you tie in the project with a real life problem "close to home." For example, for the past 31 years, this author has been visiting Mammoth Mountain located in Eastern California. Since about 1990, she has noticed dead and dying trees near Horseshoe Lake. What are the possible explanations for this? How can we slow down the process, stop further destruction, how does this affect plants, animals, and humans? Find the area or ecological system that you are familiar with and formulate questions for students' investigation.

Another example is to read Mark Twain's book *Roughing It* (New York: Harper and Brothers, 1913) where Twain refers to Mono Lake as "the dead sea of California." Ask the students to find out if Mono Lake is dead as Twain says. What methods would be appropriate to engage students to study Mono Lake (birds, alkali flies, algae, shrimp). Also find Thomas's *Mark Twain Roughed It Here* below and compare illustrations from that book with students' findings regarding the Mono Lake habitat.

Thomas, Frank J. Mark Twain roughed it here. 1st ed.
Los Angeles : Tenfingers Press, 1964.
[6] p., [8] leaves of plates : ill., 24 x 27 cm.
Subject(s): Twain, Mark, 1835-1910.
        Lakes--California--Pictorial works.
        Stencil work--Specimens.
        Mono Lake (Calif.)--Pictorial works.
Genre/form: Photographs, Original--Illustrations in books.
Location: Clark Library
Location: YRL Special Collections Call Number: F868.M67 T3

Mark Twain Roughed It Here on catalog entry

The result of students' research on the Mono Basin ecology could be presented as brief "naturalist walks" interpreting the life cycles of plants, birds, and animals, as well as descriptions of geology, water, and tufas (calcium carbonate formed by the mixing of waters of different compositions) of the Mono Lake Basin. Technologies used to produce these interpretive guides for tourists could vary from audio guides, audio and video podcasting programs, to paper handouts.

Inquiry-based learning in science research projects

The following are sample research projects in science that are scalable to different levels of students' aptitude and preference.

Ecosystem is one of these interdisciplinary approaches to science that is required to study and answer questions of organic foods, innovative materials, energy and environmental policy, disease vectors in various biomes (of plants, animals, people), and behavioral, physical, and physiological adaptations among the populations of endangered species and how to preserve them (e.g., in a temperate rainforest, say in Washington and British Columbia).

Examples of two such projects are described next. One is related to the invisible CO_2 gas killing trees at Mammoth Mountain. See sources produced by USGS <http://quake.wr.usgs.gov/VOLCANOES/LongValley/>. As one of the final projects, students may produce a podcast with information that alerts visitors about the overall CO_2 activity and write a poster to be mounted on trees about the hazardous area and rules of conduct. Another project may involve designing and developing an interpretive podcasting service for the visitors to the Mono Basin of the Inyo National Forest explaining the tufa tower formations, as well as high salt concentration supporting alkali flies, migratory birds, and brine shrimp. Students' podcasts would be reviewed by Mono Lake experts and used for visitors at rangers' stations.

For studying biomes on the Web, besides the encyclopedia—both printed and on the Web, books, almanacs, and other specialized guides—you might get started with the following sources:

- Biomes Vocabulary accessed online 8/7/06 <http://earthobservatory.nasa.gov/Laboratory/Biome/vocabulary.html>

- Earth Observatory gives a quick and excellent explanation of biomes including tundra, shrubland, rainforest, grassland, desert, and forests accessed online 8/7/06 <http://earthobservatory.nasa.gov/Laboratory/Biome/>

- The World's Biomes, developed by the Museum of Paleontology, University of California at Berkeley <http://www.ucmp.berkeley.edu/glossary/gloss5/biome/>

- Your Key to Biomes accessed online 8/7/06 <http://lsb.syr.edu/projects/cyber-zoo/biome.html>

Each of the above may be discussed in terms of the checklist for evaluation of Internet sources (see Think Guide #4 for Chapter 7).

Nano-manufacturing research, interdisciplinary in nature, promises to revolutionize homeland security, biomedicine (diagnosis, therapy), space exploration, telecommunication, and computing. Devices are at the molecular level and because of these properties, they are efficient and precise (e.g., plasmonic imaging lithography, nano-CAD, assemblage of components, also known as nano-LEGO, solar cells from nano scale titania and non-toxic dye, from the red coloring of cherries and raspberries; see Scanning Probe Microscope images <www.nanoscience.com/education/gallery.html>). For sample nanotechnology driven inquiry modules, see *Teaching Nanotechnology in the High School Curriculum: A Teacher's Guide*, by Ken Bowles, 2004.

Socialized computing: craigslist, Technorati search engine that scans millions of blogs and displays on keywords a.k.a. tags, podcasting (amateur shows typically using iPods for weaving voice, graphics, movie clips, and music), wikis (Web pages that allow users to create/edit contents without peer reviews), and RSS (really simple syndication) feeds, to mention just some of the examples. (*Technology Review*, 2006, MIT, 108(8):43) Students may select a technology, or discuss common themes that are representative of all technologies (e.g., ethical issues, specific technical solutions, user interfaces, and evaluation methods to compare these technologies for a given task).

Topics are numerous, resources are plentiful, friendlier than ever before, and many are accessible free of charge through digital libraries and portals, library Web-catalogs, and reference resources.

All projects are based on the following:

- Authentic problems that students can connect to and experience (e.g., the issue of adaptation of birds in the Mono Lake Basin)

- Multiple opportunities to study identified problems (e.g., research using software, databases, and library resources, lab instruments, observation)

- Application of sound pedagogies including "fading" scaffolding (in terms of structure and help mechanisms in facilitating the learning process)

- Linking educators' expertise and technology with the ability to scale down or up scientific inquiries at the level of students' capabilities and preferences

- Building digital clearinghouses (e.g., best practices, lesson plans and refinements, assessment instruments).

Appendix F (especially for educators)
Collaborative Sample Project in Arts

Museum interpretive guides will be developed in small groups of about three to four students per group. Art teachers in collaboration with librarians will work together to develop team projects that require a combination of visual literacy (appreciation) as well as information and technological competencies; the result will be a museum interpretive guide designed for a specific user profile (e.g., middle school students; senior citizens; intelligent lay visitors with no or little background in art history and curatorial activities).

Project description:

Visit your local museum and select a collection (exhibits) that interests you (e.g., ancient jewelry; red-figured Greek vases; 20th century photography; textiles; books of hours; contemporary art). Variations on this theme could include "Public Art at [your school name]," or "Walking Guide through Historic [your city/town]."

Each of you will assume a particular role that is important for the success of the entire project. Each student depends on the work of others in a collaborative effort. Using podcasting technology which will be introduced in class (you may choose another medium of expression such as Web pages), design and develop brief audiovisual visitors' tour guides interpreting the objects in the selected collection. Your audience will be specified in your project.

Your team roles are as follows:

(a) *museum curator* understands the collection, promotes various collections through developing special exhibits, museum catalogs, and educational programs and guides

(b) *bibliographer* is charged in selecting readings for the team as well as brief background readings for the visitors; these will be published as "further readings" in back of their guide note

(c) *technology coordinator* understands the purpose of the project, the audience, and the technology

(d) *project manager* has excellent communication and overall skills (written and oral); he or she will test the pilot project before releasing to the public, fine tune the program, and plan future activities.

There are two ways to obtain digital images of the collection you will be representing and interpreting:

Image capturing (field work scanning)

- Select a collection of museum objects of your choice;

- Explain the purpose and scope of your project; obtain the permission of the museum officials to proceed with the project;

- Obtain a set of digital images in adequate resolution (number of dots per inch, dpi); for example, in an 8-bit image, each pixel has 256 (2^8) possible colors; a 24-bit image has _____ possible colors?

- Cite the sources of images following a bibliographic style that your institution uses.

Born digital images

1. Select a virtual museum collection; this can be from commercial online databases, such as ARTstor, as well as individual museums;
   a. search the collection
   b. use tags (a.k.a. keywords or topics)
   c. modify your search to get exactly what you want
      i. migrant workers [qualified by] depression
      ii. harp player [qualified by] Ancient Greece

2. Digital images should be in the resolution range in order to produce the required quality (the higher the resolution of an image, the greater its clarity);
   a. Open the word document
   b. Search images that you have the right to download from the public domain; read information on digital rights management and intellectual property rights
   c. Right-click on the image
   d. Click on "save as" from the pull down menu and paste the image in the open word document

3. Cite the sources (see above under *image capturing*).

Description of images within a given collection

Regardless of the method you are using to produce digital images, you will need to describe or annotate each image before you provide the audio content for your guide. In fact, the following four categories may be used to describe objects in general rather than merely images. We will describe these four categories as "views."

Image_View relates to artistic and cultural values of an image:
   i. *image* itself in terms of what it is or what it *represents* (landscape, still life, portrait, religious content, early books, documentation of migrant workers, child labor)
   ii. *material* it is made of (plaster, bronze, jade, silk, parchment, marble, ivory)

iii. *technique* used to make the object (oil on canvas, charcoal, etching, watercolors, glass blowing)

iv. *physical* description (size, color)

v. *provenance* (chain of ownership and properties of the object when a given museum acquired it from previous owner)

vi. *cultural* value may be used as a piece of evidence; for example, by looking at some painted ancient Greek vessels, one can see the Trojan War heroes; we can also tell about the technology of manufacturing and time period

Creation_View relates to data elements that will hold information about names of artists who created their vases, jewelry, pottery, statuettes, pictures, fabrics, books, decorative objects, etc.

Usage_View relates to specific users that you think the object will be appropriate for, digital rights in terms of users' right to take a photo of, to download into a digital photo album, print, etc.

Collection_View relates to a broader context or collection of the object described; you may want to describe the object within a gallery (e.g., a sculpture of Aphrodite in a gallery of gods and goddesses) and within the entire collection (e.g., antiquities of Greece and Rome).

These four views, object_view, creation_view, usage_view, and collection_view, may be described with 15 properties of the Dublin Core <http://dublincore.org> including data elements such as contributor, coverage, creator, date, description, format, language, publisher, rights, subject, title, abstract, audience, and availability. Table F1 below gives some of the properties associated with four View_Types.

View_Type	Properties (values)
Object_View	artifact itself, material, techniques, physical description, provenance
Creation_View	creator, place of creation, date
Usage_View	audience, availability, digital rights
Collection_View	description of its immediate collection—panoramic_view; wide-angle_view collection.

Table F1: Describing image objects in a given collection

Helpful Resources:

The three thesauri (or dictionaries designed to facilitate indexing and searching of art related collections) are all produced by Getty. You may want to use words and phrases as descriptive tags for images (also known as "falksonomy" as the tags are given by searchers or users of collections).

Art & Architecture Thesaurus
<www.getty.edu/research/conducting_research/vocabularies/aat/>

Thesaurus of Geographic Names
<www.getty.edu/research/conducting_research/vocabularies/tgn/>

Union List of Artist Names
<www.getty.edu/research/conducting_research/vocabularies/ulan/>

ARTstor <www.artstor.org> is a digital library of about 400,000 art images from a wide range of cultures and time periods. This image database may be searched by words or phrases (e.g. from title, creator, subject); alternatively, you may want first to explore the contents of the database by browsing the collections. The result will be thumbnail images. To view the image record, click on the caption; double-click on the thumbnail to open the Image Viewer, which facilitates zooming, downloading, and printing.

All this will be separately described and explained to you by your classroom instructor. ARTstor was initiated in 2000 and modeled on the Mellon Foundation's support of the JSTOR journal-archive project.

Appendix G (especially for educators)
Sample Projects in Social Sciences

Introduction

National Council for the Social Studies (NCSS) <http://www.ncss.org/standards/> recommends the following 10 thematic strands in social sciences as a framework for educators, administrators, and stakeholders in the K-12 grade educational settings; these are:

- Culture
- Time, continuity, and change
- People, places, and environments
- Individual development and identity
- Individuals, groups, and institutions
- Power, authority, and governance
- Production, distribution, and consumption
- Science, technology, and society
- Global connections
- Civil ideals and practices

In addition, projects would want to consider Information Literacy Standards, *Standards for the 21st-Century Learner* (AASL, 2007) as well as ISTE's National Educational Technology Standards for Students <http://www.iste.org/standards>. This three-prong approach should be interwoven into lesson plans, projects, and learning experiences throughout the educational process. However, not all standards need to be always present in each of the projects. For example, a history project might include several strands from NCSS, and several from NETS-S. All projects should engage students in practicing critical thinking skills, applying knowledge to new situations, collaborating, sharing, and using knowledge responsibly and productively.

Specific topics along these broad social science strands may include topics such as:

i. representation of hippies in current television and film
ii. "pop" art in the sixties
iii. perceptions of the Vietnam War in the United States
iv. the origins of radical feminism in the 1960s
v. the Black Power Movement in Los Angeles, 1965-1975
vi. American Jewish youth in the sixties
vii. Harlem Renaissance, Chicago jazz, and so on

For these and other topics in United States history within the strands identified above, there are excellent printed and digital sources to explore. In any research assignment, you will want to include a wide variety of resources including books, maps, videos, sound recordings, articles from magazines and journals, as well as primary sources that we have just described.

Consulting general and specialized encyclopedias, and proceeding to books, films, CDs, and DVDs seems to be the norm for any successful research project. In order to check the location of various sources, you will search your library catalogs. It will describe those materials that your library has with regard to books, DVDs, maps, CDs, and other special materials. The exception is periodical literature. Access to articles has been the responsibility of online databases such as EBSCOhost, ProQuest, SIRS, InfoTrac, CultureGrams online, JSTOR, ARTstor, CQ Press databases, and others. Check your library to find out what resources they subscribe to.

In addition to published sources, we have annotated some of the excellent digital libraries for you to get started:

American Memory at the Library of Congress: <http://memory.loc.gov> from there students will explore various collections such as the one from the Prints and Photographs Division of the Library of Congress: <http://memory.loc.gov/ammem/daghtml/daghome.html>

History Matters (George Mason University) <http://www.historymatters.gmu.edu> contains primary documents, images, interviews, and annotated Web sites of American history.

Our Documents <http://www.ourdocuments.gov> is a collaboration among National History Day, the National Archives, and Records Administration (NARA) <http://www.archives.gov> and has assembled milestone documents in American history.

The Gilder Lehrman Institute of American History <http://gilderlehrman.org> contains more than 60,000 documents detailing abolitionism, expansion, and feminism.

Making of America <http://www.hti.umich.edu/m/moagrp/> is a digital library of primary sources in American history with more than 50,000 journal articles and 9,000 books with 19th century imprints.

Appendix H1:

The Dewey Decimal Classification

000 GENERALITIES
010 Bibliographies & catalogs
020 Library & information sciences
030 General encyclopedic works
040 Unassigned
050 General serials & their indexes
060 General organizations & museology
070 News media, journalism, publishing
080 General collections
090 Manuscripts & rare books

100 PHILOSOPHY & PSYCHOLOGY
110 Metaphysics
120 Epistemology, causation, humankind
130 Paranormal phenomena
140 Specific philosophical schools
150 Psychology
160 Logic
170 Ethics (Moral philosophy)
180 Ancient, medieval, oriental philosophy
190 Modern Western philosophy

200 RELIGION
210 Natural theology
220 Bible
230 Christian theology
240 Christian moral & devotional theology
250 Christian orders & local churches
260 Christian social theology
270 Christian church history
280 Christian denominations & sects
290 Other and comparative religions

300 SOCIAL SCIENCES
310 General statistics
320 Political science
330 Economics
340 Law
350 Public administration
360 Social services; associations
370 Education
380 Commerce, communication, transport
390 Customs, etiquette, folklore

400 LANGUAGE
410 Linguistics
420 English & old English
430 Germanic languages
440 Romance languages
450 Italian, Romanian, Rhaeto-Romanic languages
460 Spanish & Portuguese languages

470 Italic languages, i.e., Latin
480 Hellenic languages, i.e., Classical Greek
490 Other languages

500 NATURAL SCIENCES & MATHEMATICS
510 Mathematics
520 Astronomy & allied sciences
530 Physics
540 Chemistry & allied sciences
550 Earth sciences
560 Paleontology, Paleozoology
570 Life sciences
580 Botanical sciences
590 Zoological sciences

600 TECHNOLOGY (Applied Sciences)
610 Medical sciences
620 Engineering & allied sciences
630 Agriculture
640 Management & auxiliary services
650 Chemical engineering
660 Home economics & family living
670 Manufacturing
680 Manufacture for specific uses
690 Buildings

700 THE ARTS
710 Civic & landscape art
720 Architecture
730 Plastic arts
740 Drawing & decorative arts
750 Painting & paintings
760 Graphic arts
770 Music
780 Photography & photographs
790 Recreational & performing arts

800 LITERATURE & RHETORIC
810 American literature in English
820 English and Old English literature
830 Literatures of Germanic languages
840 Literatures of Romance languages
850 Italian, Romanian, Rhaeto-Romanic
860 Spanish & Portuguese literatures
870 Italic literatures, i.e., Latin
880 Hellenic literatures, i.e., Classical Greek
890 Literatures of other languages

900 GEOGRAPHY & HISTORY
910 Geography & travel
920 Biography, Genealogy, Insignias
930 History of the ancient world
940 General history of Europe
950 General history of Asia & Far East
960 General history of Africa
970 General history of North America
980 General history of South America
990 General history of other areas

Dewey Decimal Classification organizes library materials in the 10 classes outlined at <http://www.tnrdlib.bc.ca/dewey.html>.

Appendix H2:

Mapping Dewey Decimal Classification (DDC) to Library of Congress Classification (LCC)

While schools and many public libraries organize their collections according to DDC, college libraries use LCC to organize their collections. Our point of departure is DDC as you will want to explore your school and public libraries first before you search college libraries. The chart below maps main classes from DDC to LCC.

DDC	Ten Classes	LC	Classification
000	Generalities	A	General Works
		Z	Bibliography, Library Science & Information Sources
100	Philosophy & Psychology	B	Philosophy
		BC	Logic
		BF	Psychology
200	Religion	BL	Religion
300	Social Sciences	H	Social Sciences
320	Political science	J	Political Sciences
340	Law	K	Law
370	Education	L	Education
400	Languages	P	Language and Literature
500	Natural Sciences &	Q	Science
510	Mathematics	QA	Mathematics
600	Technology	T	Technology (general)
610	Medicine	R	Medicine
630		S	Agriculture
		U	Military Science
		V	Naval Science
700	The Arts	N	Fine Arts
780	Music	M	Music
800	Literature and Rhetoric	P	Language and Literature
900	Geography & History	G	Geography (general), atlases, maps
		C	Auxiliary sciences of history
		D	History: Europe, Asia, Africa
		E-F	History: America

Table H1: A DDC to LCC crosswalk

Appendix I:

Pre-Test: A Baseline for Information Literacy Skills

Pretend you are getting ready for your trip to _____.
You own a good map of the city.

Besides the map, what else do you need to know about your trip?
List the three most important things (for you) that you would want to know.

How would you go about finding these three things?

Question #1: (I'd need/like to know ...)

Answer #1: Where would you find this information?

Question #2: (I'd like to know . . .)

Answer #2: Where would you find this information?

Question #3: (I'd like to ...)

Answer #3: Where would you find this information?

Please return this sheet with your answers to me
THANK YOU

Appendix J:

Scoring Rubrics: Examples for Information Literacy Projects

Score Point
4

CRITERIA FOR SCORING INFORMATION LITERACY
Exceeds expectations

Student identifies at least 5 main topics (see list of topics).

Student shows understanding of content knowledge for each topic.

Student demonstrates depth of understanding (e.g., uses specific facts, examples, vocabulary).

All topics are described or discussed accurately.

Vocabulary is used accurately.

Related information is connected (e.g., credit giving, no plagiarism).

The writing is organized around main ideas (e.g., idea per paragraph).

Student gives insights/observations of his/her own.

Answers are well written.

Student is creative in presentation and title page selection.

There are few spelling errors.

3   **Meets expectations**

Student identifies at least 3-4 main topics (see list of topics).

Student shows understanding of content knowledge for each topic.

All topics are described and discussed accurately.

Related information is connected (e.g., credit giving, plagiarism).

Student's writing skills need some improvement; the message is clear.

There are a number of spelling errors.

2   **Close to expectations**

Student identifies at least 3 topics.

Student shows understanding of content knowledge for each topic.

Student demonstrates depth of understanding.

All topics are described and discussed accurately.

Student's writing skills need major improvement (revision, etc.).

There are a number of spelling errors, grammatical problems, etc.

1   **Does not meet expectations**

Student demonstrates little content understanding; lists 2 topics and misses major ones.

Student gives some inaccurate or irrelevant answers or examples.

Student has numerous problems with writing, spelling, and structure.

- Information Literacy major topics, below, are presented over a 4-5 week period for 2 hours a week, 14 hours total.

1. Finding books in library; classification and DDC
2. Searching library catalogs
3. Use of encyclopedias, both printed and on the Web
4. Variety of printed and online sources
5. The Web, its use, critical thinking
6. Ethics in research, understanding attribution and practice of citing (writing bibliographies; understanding intellectual property, honor code, plagiarism)
7. Why evaluate
8. Search strategies: definition and examples from different media and sources
9. Controlling the search: search modification
10. Data elements in catalog entry
11. Differences between subject headings and keyword searching (introducing del.icio.us, flickr, zotero)
12. Library rules, Fair Use Policy
13. Research practice and general rules of thumb

- Instructional strategies: short lecture followed by a project-based, guided hands-on collaborative activities in small teams of two students in a group. Setting may be a library, computer labs, or wired classrooms.

Appendix K:

Post-Test: An Example for Take Home Final Quiz

Write an essay that includes as many information literacy topics that every 11th grade student should learn and know. You may want to select the most important and interesting topics to you that are covered in your library research units. Since this is a take home assignment, you may use any material to help you write the essay (as you did during the open book quizzes in school).

Instructions:

Make a front cover and include the following three things:
- Give a title to your essay paper
- Put your name (last and first) on the front cover
- Write the date when you completed this essay

Instructions for the essay:

- Type your paper and run spellcheck before you turn in
- The paper should be not less than 2 full pages and not more than 3 pages in length
- You can include bibliography: 1-2 entries at the end of your paper following one of the bibliographic style manuals (OPTIONAL)
- Write clearly using full sentences; write your essay into several paragraphs: an idea = one paragraph. Be imaginative and have fun!

Appendix L:

Online Databases: A Checklist for Evaluating Online Services

This Appendix has two parts: Part One contains a checklist that instructors can use as a tool for evaluating, comparing, and contrasting online database services. Part Two briefly summarizes ProQuest, JSTOR, EBSCOhost, InfoTrac, CQ Electronic library, and SIRS services. This certainly is a partial list of online database services that many schools consider and subscribe to. Many other online systems are not included here.

Part One: Checklist for evaluating Web-ready online databases for schools

1. Scope and sense of one's space in a given system
    1.1 What is the breadth of the database? For example, how many journals, newspapers, and magazines are regularly indexed in the database?
    1.2 What is the depth of the database? For example, how many scholarly periodical titles are included? Are there any of popular nature, of technical orientation?
    1.3 What else is included in the database? Examples may be reference books, reports, and if so, who produces them?
    1.4 What is the time coverage of the database or parts of it?
    1.5 How current is the database? Some think that if the service is online it is more current than printed services; this may not be true.
    1.6 Which languages are represented besides English? Examples may be Spanish, French newspapers, reports, and so forth.
    1.7 Is there a special description or explanation about inclusion policy or indexing policy? Can you as a teacher or librarian suggest materials to be included or considered in the database?
    1.8 How aligned is the content to middle school curriculum? To high school curriculum, college-level programs?
    1.9 How integrated is the content with regard to textbooks and standards for a particular grade level?
    1.10 Is the content self-explanatory?

2. Ease of using a given database
    2.1 What kinds of tutorials are available for high school students?
    2.2 How much extra teaching do we have to invest in order to teach students in the use of a given database?

2.3   Is the system (online database) forgiving? This may be viewed at several levels: typographic errors, syntax, reminders, and so forth.

3.   User interface criteria (defined as anything that the user comes in contact with, physically, cognitively, perceptually)

   3.1   How well are the screens labeled?

   3.2   Is the layout designed consistently?

   3.3   Is the system free of library terminology (jargon)?

4.   System complexity: access and vocabulary issues

   4.1   How is the database organized?

   4.2   Are there vocabulary lists that may be useful in searching?

   4.3   Is the level of specificity in subject lists useful to high school students?

   4.4   How does the vocabulary list compare with the level of specificity of their project topics?

Part Two: Summary of ProQuest databases:

ProQuest's users can select from the main menu "all databases" or one of the following choices:

- ProQuest Platinum covers 2,363 magazine and journal titles, of which more than 1,000 are full-text, or 43 percent (as of June 2007); of these about 500 are especially applicable to 7-12 grade students.
- CultureGrams (Online World Edition)
- International Newspapers with 37 English language papers
- ProQuest Historical Newspapers with full-text coverage of major papers such as:
  - *The New York Times* (1851-2003)
  - *The Wall Street Journal* (1889-1989)
  - *The Washington Post* (1877-1990)
  - *The Christian Science Monitor* (1908-1993)
  - *The Los Angeles Times* (1881-1985)
- SIRS Researcher® and other databases (explained separately below)
- Reference sources include *World Book Encyclopedia*
- The Ethnic Cultures of America

The ProQuest Platinum may be searched in two different modes: the basic search option as well as the advanced. You can access articles by knowing publication titles (e.g., *Science News*) in which you know that a desired article appeared, as well as by browsing broad categories (e.g., Arts & Humanities, subdivided into art, history, literature, music, performing arts, etc.). Both keyword and subject headings are used to index and describe the articles. Use "quotation marks" to search exact phrases. The database uses AND, OR, and NOT Boolean operators for combining search terms. The wildcard symbol* is used as a right-handed truncation character while the symbol ? replaces any single character, either inside the word or the right end of the word. Articles may be printed, e-mailed, or exported for future reference. For search tips, go online at <http://proquest.umi.com/i-std/en/pri/>. Please refer to Chapter 8 for details on how to search ProQuest.

Contact information for ProQuest:
Telephone: (800) 247-7198
fax: 734-662-4554
Internet: <http://proquest.umi.com>

Summary of JSTOR resources:

JSTOR is a non-profit archive containing full-text high resolution scanned images of scholarly articles, beginning with the first issue of each periodical title. There is typically a five-year gap between a journal's most recently published issue and the content available through JSTOR. This "moving wall" is changing. Some journals date as far back as the 1600s. JSTOR is searched by means of keywords, which are then compared with words from the title, author, citation, and the body of the article. You may combine keywords using the Boolean operators AND, OR, and NOT.

For more search tips, visit JSTOR online search tutorial at:
<http://www.jstor.org/help/search.html>

Contact information for JSTOR User Services:
301 East Liberty Suite 250
Ann Arbor, MI 48104-2262
Telephone: (734) 998-9101
Fax: (734) 998-9113
Email: support@jstor.org

Summary of EBSCOhost databases:

Student Research Center <http://web.ebscohost.com/src/> features the following:
- Basic and advanced search capabilities
- *American Heritage Dictionary* (4th ed.)
- *Columbia Encyclopedia*
- Teacher Resources
- Top searches (popular topics such as hurricanes, global warming, March Madness)
- Spotlight topic (e.g., National Women's History Month was featured in April 2007)
- Searching by topic, where topics are arranged hierarchically (e.g., English & language Arts are subdivided into Authors, Children's Literature, English Literature, Folklore & Myths, Journalism, Literary Criticism, Plays, World Literature, etc.)

- Searching may be limited by date range, reading level, and full-text article
- Keywords and subject headings may be used to access articles
- Any or all of the following formats may be included (e.g., magazines, newspapers, books and encyclopedias, biographies, radio and television news transcripts, country reports, state/province reports, primary sources, and photos and maps)

Contact information for EBSCOhost:
United States and Canada: (800) 653-2726
International: (978) 356-6500
Fax: (978) 356-6565

Summary of CQ Electronic Library:

CQ Electronic Library is published by CQ Press, a Division of Congressional Quarterly, Inc. The CQ Electronic Library includes the following online resources:
- *The CQ Researcher Online*
- *CQ Congress Collection*
- *CQ Supreme Court Collection*
- *CQ Encyclopedia of American Government*
- *CQ Congress and the Nation Online Edition*
- *CQ Weekly*
- *CQ Public Affairs Collection*
- *CQ Voting and Elections Collection*
- *CQ California Political Almanac*
- *CQ Historic Document Series Online Edition*
- *CQ Supreme Court Yearbook Online Edition*
- *CQ Washington Information Directory Online Edition*
- *CQ Vital Statistics on American Politics Online Edition*

Contact information for CQ Press:
1255 22nd Street N.W.
Washington, DC 20037
Telephone: (800) 834-9020 x1822
Internet: <http://library.cqpress.com>

Summary of SIRS databases for schools:

SIRS offers four main databases that can be purchased annually; these are:

- **SIRS Researcher** is a general database that contains full-text articles from more than 1,200 publications worldwide. These are searchable by three search methods: by means of using Subject Headings Search, Topic Browse, and Keyword Search. The CD-ROM version contains excerpts from *The World Almanac* and *Book of Facts* (1998). There are maps as well. The Web version includes *Today's News*—headline news stories updated hourly, dictionary and thesaurus.

- **SIRS Discoverer** is an interactive reference tool for young researchers, with articles from more than 450 publications; this database is searchable via Subject Tree, Keyword Search, and Subject Heading Search.

- **SIRS Government Reporter** contains full-text government documents and recent U.S. Supreme Court decisions on a wide variety of topics. This database is searchable through Subject Tree Search, Subject Headings Search, Department/Agency Browse, Keyword Search, Country Profile Browse and Census Bureau Browse.

- **SIRS Renaissance** contains full-text articles from 500 sources in the Arts & Humanities. The database is cumulative and updated every February and September. Search methods include: Subject Tree, Subject Headings Search, and Keyword Search.

Contact information for SIRS Knowledge Source database <http://sks.sirs.com> is via ProQuest.
Telephone: (800) 232-SIRS
Fax: (561) 994-4704
Internet: <www.sirs.com>

Gale Cengage's Literature Resource Center includes:

- Biographical entries on more than 130,000 authors, from *Contemporary Authors*, *Contemporary Authors New Revisions*, *Dictionary of Literary Biography*, *Contemporary Literary Criticism,* and other Gale sources, providing detailed biographical, bibliographical, and contextual information about authors' lives and works

- More than 70,000 selected full-text critical essays and reviews from Contemporary Literary Criticism, Classical and Medieval Literature Criticism, Literature Criticism from 1400-1800, Nineteenth-Century Literature Criticism, Twentieth-Century Literary Criticism, as well as Drama Criticism, Poetry Criticism, Shakespearean Criticism, Short Story Criticism, and Children's Literature Review

- More than 7,000 overviews of frequently studied works, from sources including Gale's For Students series, Literature and Its Times and Characters in 20th-Century Fiction

- More than 650,000 full-text articles, critical essays, and reviews from more than 300 scholarly journals and literary magazines

- Nearly 30,000 full-text poems, short stories, plays, and more than 4,500 interviews

- The ability to identify groups of authors who share characteristics such as genre, time period, themes, nationality, ethnicity and gender

- *Merriam-Webster's® Encyclopedia of Literature*

Literature Resource Center subscribers can choose to add any of the following products as fully integrated modules:

- Scribner Writers Series, a collection of more than 2,200 original, detailed bio-critical essays on the lives and works of important authors from around the world
- Twayne's Authors Series, featuring the content of nearly 600 books in three print series. This series offers in depth introductions to the lives and works of writers, the history and influence of literary movements, and the development of literary genres
- The Modern Language Association (MLA) International Bibliography. Literature Resource Center subscribers who add the MLA International Bibliography also get the MLA International Bibliography on InfoTrac as a standalone database at no extra cost.

GALE CENGAGE Learning
P.O. Box 9187
Farmington Hills, MI 48333-9187
Telephone: (800) 877-GALE
Fax: (800) 414-0504
Internet: <www.gale.com>

Appendix M:

Self-Reflection: Getting Insight into Students' Level of Awareness

Self-reflection consist of questions intended to assess students' awareness and perception of the level of planning, cognitive strategy, self-checking, and awareness during a problem solving task (O'Neil & Abedi). These questions are given to students in situations of testing, and may be extended to Web searching, research report preparation, and similar situations.

PLANNING

COGNITIVE STRATEGY

SELF-CHECKING

AWARENESS

We link questions to applications that are specific to information literacy tasks.

PLANNING

I tried to understand the goals of the test questions before I attempted to answer.
I tried to determine what the test required.
I made sure I understood just what had to be done and how to do it.
I determined how to solve the test questions.
I tried to understand the test questions before I attempted to solve them.

Application to IL tasks:

Most of the high school students are assigned class projects (GOAL) that they need to achieve and produce by a certain time on a specified topic(s). The teacher typically hands out the assigned project (take home test, term paper) in a form of a written requirement that students need to meet. MEANS to achieve the goal are not specified.

The PLANNING consists first of understanding what exactly is required before investing time and effort (going to library, spending time to locate, read, take notes, analyze, evaluate, cite, etc.). Second, the overall research planning is needed as a blueprint of what will actually be done in the research process. At this point, students might want to get teachers' approval before they proceed with their research process. Once approved of, students will design a finer plan in order to find and locate the best information sources for the assigned project. Search strategy as well as the road map in Figure 1.7 may help in the planning phase.

> **COGNITIVE STRATEGY**
>
> I attempted to discover the main ideas in the questions.
> I asked myself how the test questions related to what I already knew.
> I thought through the meaning of the test questions before I began to answer them.
> I used multiple thinking techniques or strategies to solve the test question.
> I selected and organized relevant information to solve the test questions.

Application to IL:

What are the sub-strategies for specific systems?
What do I need to have and know in order to search the library catalog (vocabulary of the domain knowledge; conceptual preparation; mechanics of searching specific systems—they are all different; do I use connectors and which ones?)

> **SELF-CHECKING**
>
> I checked my work while I was doing it.
> I corrected my errors.
> I almost always knew how much of the test I had left to complete.
> I kept track of my progress and, if necessary, I changed my techniques or strategies.
> I checked my accuracy as I progressed through the test.

Application to IL:

How am I doing? (both print, online, the Web)?
Any good sites (exploit those and get more good sites)?
Getting zero results—what does that mean? Which errors did I make?
How can I fix these errors? What types of errors? Typographic errors, wrong words, wrong syntax, wrong database?
Do I know where I am, what I am searching (content)?
Do I need to modify my search: narrow down, or expand search to get more results?

> **AWARENESS**
>
> I was aware of my thinking.
> I was aware of which thinking technique or strategy to use and when to use it.
> I was aware of the need to plan my course of action.
> I was aware of my ongoing thinking process.
> I was aware of my trying to understand the test questions before I attempted to solve them.

Appendix N:

Summarizing Sources

There are four basic rules to remember whenever you annotate documents that you used in your reports:

- Use your own words and not the authors' words. Making changes, such as word variants, synonymous words and phrases, and changing word direction, does not count. These remain the authors' words. Teachers know how to recognize your language from your parents', authors', even your older brothers' and sisters'. So, stick to your own words and understanding of the work you wish to cite and include in your bibliography.

- Mention highlights only rather than everything that is discussed in the document you are annotating. Separate important things from less important ones; be selective. If you are given 2-3 sentences only to summarize a work, what would it look like?

- Be critical of others' writings in a positive way.

- Include, as much as you wish, your own insight and understanding; make connections.

How to summarize (annotate) an article: an example

> Raymer, Steve. 1993. St. Petersburg, capital of the tsars. *National Geographic* 184 (6): 96-121.

Summary: Monument to the worldly aspirations of its namesake rule and his imperial successors, St. Petersburg (also known as Petrograd, or City of Peter, as well as Leningrad) has survived the communist years to rival Moscow as Russia's cultural center. The article also shows historical and city maps of the city. In terms of **organization**, the article is typical of other magazine stories. It traces the city's rich and turbulent history since its birth in 1703, Russia's triumph over Napoleon in 1812, and the 1917 revolution. Special **features** are photographs of lavish mosaics gracing the Church of the Resurrection, ornate facades and opulent interiors of palaces, museums, theaters, and parks. The author uses a popular style of writing, with pictures of gleaming ballrooms, libraries, and gardens of the tsars of Russia. Steve Raymer, who is the author of the book *St. Petersburg*, is both writer and photographer.

Summarizing your Sources on Your Own

> Citation

Summary:

Issues or questions the work raises:

Special features of the work (index, resources, illustrations, interviews, pictures, portraits, primary sources such as manuscripts and diaries, statistical tables):

Organization:

Currency, multiple perspectives presented, detected bias, evidence, references

How relevant is this work to your project (is intended audience mentioned in the preface or introduction)?

Appendix O:
Cited Reference Printed Sources

Manuals of Bibliographic Style
Gibaldi, Joseph. MLA Handbook for Writers of Research Papers. 6th ed. New York: Modern
    Language Association of America, 2003.
Publication Manual of the American Psychological Association. 5th ed. Washington, DC:
    American Psychological Association, 2001.
Turabian, K. L. *A Manual for Writers of Term Papers, Theses, and Dissertations: Chicago
    style for students and researchers.* 7th ed. Rev. by Wayne C. Booth, Gregory G.
    Colomb, Joseph M. Williams, and University of Chicago Press editorial staff. Chicago:
    University of Chicago Press, 2007.

"Desk" or "College" Dictionaries
The American Heritage College Dictionary. 4th ed. Boston: Houghton Mifflin, 2007.
Webster's Ninth New Collegiate Dictionary. Rev. ed. Springfield, Mass.: Merriam-Webster, 2001.

Unabridged Dictionaries
Oxford English Dictionary. J. Simpson and E. Sdmund Weiner, eds. 2nd ed. Oxford:
    Clarendon Press, 1989, 20 vols. Supplements.
Webster's Third New International Dictionary of the English Language, unabridged. Philip
    Babcock Gove and the Merriam-Webster editorial staff. Springfield, Mass.: Merriam-
    Webster, 2002.

Subject or Technical Dictionaries
Allaby, M. *Dictionary of the Environment.* 3rd ed. New York: New York University Press, 1989.
Dorland's Illustrated Medical Dictionary. 30th ed. Philadelphia, Pa.: Saunders, 2003.
The New Grove Dictionary of Music and Musicians. Stanley Sadie, ed.; executive editor, John
    Tyrrell. 2nd ed. New York: Grove, 2001. 29 vols.

Slang Dictionaries
Chapman, Robert L., ed. *New Dictionary of American Slang.* New York: Harper & Collins,
    1998.
Partridge, Eric, ed. *New Partridge Dictionary of Slang and Unconventional English.*
    London: Routledge, 2006. 2 vols.

Synonyms and Antonyms
Roget's International Thesaurus. 6th ed. New York: HarperCollins, 2001.

General and Comprehensive Encyclopedias
Encyclopedia Americana. The International ed. Danbury, Conn.: Scholastic Library Pub.,
    2006. 30 vols.
The New Encyclopedia Britannica, 15th ed. Chicago: Encyclopedia Britannica, 2002, 32 vols.
The World Book Encyclopedia. 2007 ed. Chicago, Ill.: World Book, 2007. 22 vols.

Subject Encyclopedias

McGraw-Hill Encyclopedia of Science & Technology. 10th ed. New York: McGraw-Hill, 2007. 20 vols.

The New Palgrave: A Dictionary of Economics. New York: Stockton Press, 1998. 4 vols.

Almanacs, Yearbooks, Handbooks, Directories

Bartlett's Familiar Quotations: A Collection of Passages, Phrases and Proverbs Traced to Their Sources in Ancient and Modern Literature. John Bartlett, ed.; Justin Kaplan, gen. ed. 17th ed. Boston, Mass.: Little, Brown, 2002.

Handbook of Chemistry and Physics. 1st Student ed., 1988. Boca Raton, Fla: Chemical Rubber Company Press, 1913- .

Information Please Almanac. Boston: Houghton Mifflin, 1974- .

Kane, Joseph N. *Famous First Facts*, 4th ed. New York: H. W. Wilson, 1997.

Statesman's Year-Book. New York: St. Martin's Press, 1864- .

World Almanac and Book of Facts. New York: World Almanac, 1868- .

Specialized Handbooks, Manuals

Consumer's Resource Handbook, 1992 ed. Washington D.C.: United States Office of Consumer Affairs, 1992.

Masterplots: 1,801 plot stories and critical evaluations of the world's finest literature/edited by Frank N. Magill; story editor, rev. ed., Dayton Kohler. Rev. 2nd ed. Pasadena, Calif.: Salem Pess, 1996. 12 vols. Expanded and updated version of the 1976 rev. ed.

Maps, Atlases, Gazetteers

Maps are produced by numerous governmental and private publishers (e.g., the U.S. Geological Survey, Central Intelligence Agency, AAA, National Geographic, Rand McNally, H. M. Gousha, General Drafting, Hammond).

Chambers World Gazetteer: *A Geographical Dictionary*. Cambridge: Cambridge University Press, 1990.

Historical Atlas of the United States. Mark C. Carnes, ed.; cartography, Malcolm A. Swanston. New York: Routledge, 2003.

National Geographic Atlas of the World, 6th rev. ed. Washington, D.C.: National Geographic Society, 1992. [medium-size world]

Rand McNally *New Cosmopolitan World Atlas, census/environmental ed*. Chicago: Rand McNally, 1991. [medium-size]

Biographical Sources:

Contemporary Authors, 1981-. New revision series. Detroit: Gale Research,

U.S. General and Specialized Sources

American Men & Women of Science: A biographical directory of today's leaders in physical, biological and related sciences, 23rd ed. Farmington Hills, Mich.: Thomson Gale, 2007.

Who's Who in America, 1899- . Chicago, Ill.: A. N. Marquis. Biennial.

World General Sources of Deceased Persons

Dictionary of Scientific Biography. New York: Scribner, 1970-1990. 8 vols. Supplements.

Webster's New Biographical Dictionary. Springfield, Mass.: Merriam-Webster, 1988.

U.S. General and Specialized Sources of Deceased Persons

Biographical Directory of the American Congress, 1774-1996. Alexandria, Va.: CQ Staff
  Directories, Inc., 1997.

Dictionary of American Biography. New York: Scribner, 1973-1994.

Notable American Women, 1607-1950. A biographical dictionary. Cambridge, Mass.:
  Belknap Press of Harvard University Press, 1971, 3 vols. Supplements.

Searching for Reviews Online

<http://www.ala.org/booklist/index.html>

<http://www.nybooks.com/nyrev/index.html>

<http://www.latimes.com/features/books/>

<http://www.nytimes.com/pages/books/index.html>

ProQuest platinum database (by subscription, see Chapter 8)

Literary Criticism

Contemporary Literary Criticism. 2nd ed. New York: Longman, 1989.

Masterplots: 2010 plot stories & essay reviews from the world's fine literature, rev. ed. Frank
  N. Magill, ed. Englewood Cliffs, N.J.: Salem Press, 1976. 12 vols.

The Novel

American Novelists since World War II. Seventh series/James R. Giles and Wanda H. Giles,
  eds. Detroit, Mich.: Gale Group, 2003.

The Columbia Granger's Index to Poetry in Anthologies. Tessa Kale, ed. 13th ed., completely
  rev., indexing anthologies published through May 31, 2006. New York: Columbia
  University Press, 2007.

Contemporary Novelists. Preface to the seventh edition, David Madden, Neil Schlager and
  Josh Lauer, eds. 7th ed. Detroit : London : St. James, 2001.

Essay and General Literature Index. New York: Wilson, 1934- . Semiannual.

General Science Index. Bronx, N.Y.: Wilson, 1978- . Monthly.

Humanities Index. Bronx, N.Y.: Wilson, 1974- . Monthly.

Play Index. Bronx, N.Y.: Wilson Company, 1952- . Irregular.

Readers' Guide to Periodical Literature. Bronx, N.Y.: Wilson, 1901-.

Short Story Index. Bronx, N.Y.: Wilson, 1953- . Annual

Song Index. Edited by Minnie Earl Sears. [n. p.] Shoe String Press, 1966.

Appendix P:
Evaluation of Sources

Evaluation of sources—of particular interest to teachers, parents, and to anyone who wishes to buy reference books

Once we have identified and located items of interest, especially through informal channels, remote catalogs, and bibliographies on the Web, such as Worldcat <www.worldcat.org> and Amazon <www.amazon.com>, we need to evaluate these sources, both reference and topical. For the coverage of reference sources, readers are referred to Chapters 4 and 5. We list reviewing sources in this section because these are important titles for teachers, parents, and anyone who wishes to buy a dictionary, almanac, encyclopedia, or any other reference book. We also assume that experienced teachers are well versed in matters of the selection process in general, and intellectual freedom, in particular. Other interesting and controversial topics include the meaning of collection development in a time of global information access, where an e-book (electronic book) may be competing with a p-book (printed book) in the near future.

The well known bibliographic sources include *American Historical Fiction*, *Senior High School Catalog*, and *Subject Guide to Books for Intermediate Grades*. Other reviewing sources include: *Booklist, Horn Book, Journal of Youth Services in Libraries* (the Association for Library Service to Children, Young Adult Library Services Association), *Library Journal, School Library Journal*, and *School Library Media Quarterly* (Journal of the American Association of School Libraries).

Why evaluate? First, not everything that you have managed to retrieve will be equally valuable to your interest, or reliable in content. Of the potentially relevant items, you need to sift through the information based on authority, and artistic and literary excellence. Second, there might be a wealth of information that you cannot use directly in your work; for example, the material is too expensive to obtain, or it is outdated or difficult to understand.

Reference sources, as defined earlier, have a purpose to rapidly locate a book, to show tables of statistical data and various distributions in a particular place and time, to give information about schools, people, services, and so on. These pieces of information are typically not related to one another in the way individual chapters in a novel or a report are. For example, words in a dictionary are arranged alphabetically rather than by their meaning. Therefore, reference sources are used differently from **topical sources** due to differences in their main intent and **structure.** Topical sources, such as novels, newspaper and magazine articles, tell a story in a certain way, develop characters in a story, evoke a particular mood or scenery, describe experiments, and draw conclusions. A reader responds to this accordingly: it is natural to read a novel in a linear fashion, from one chapter to the next starting with the first chapter, in the order written by its author. Because the structure of reference sources is made up of files, entries, and data elements, people scan through selective entries only; they do not read entries sequentially from cover-to-cover. These characteristics of reference sources are important to keep in mind throughout the evaluation process.

One of the most important points to consider is the **preface,** often referred to as an introduction. It describes selection criteria, the organization of a work, its content, special features, and how to use it.

Next to consider is the **author's name** and the **title page** of a source. Both are applicable for printed and electronic sources regardless of their form (e.g., dictionary, directory, almanac, magazine title, as well as books and journal articles). The **author/creator** may be a person, a group of people, an editor, an agency, or a publisher. Some publishers, including government bodies, are well established producers of reports and other materials.

Special attention should be given to **the title page** as it gives the fullest amount of information for the purposes of identification, citing, and evaluation. The title page may also contain the title and subtitle of the source as well as an edition statement. The publication date is equally important to consider. As a rule of thumb, use the most current edition of a work, especially when evaluating reference sources. Other elements that you will typically find on a title page are the name of the publisher and the place of publication. Finally, check the sources that were used in the process of compiling the reference work. This is especially important to pay attention to when using Web-based reference sources. Is the Web version an abridged version of the full work? Is it updated as often as its printed source, or does it serve as a promotional material to sell its full source? Equally important are bibliographic entries, sometimes with annotations, as well as an index to the entire work.

Index